Strategies

in

Defence and Intelligence

Attention Authors

Manas Publications is fighting a war to tell the world that India can win the battle not only by bullet but also by pen. We are converting fighters into writers as there is no dearth of intellectuals in our country but their knowledge is confined to them only. No sincere effort has been made by any other publisher to give right direction to their knowledge and the talent of every intellectual is lying hidden. An author always gives the raw material in the shape of a manuscript and it depends upon the publisher how to make it a finished product. We are motivating the intellectuals' mind and publishing their manuscripts for more than two decades and would like to publish your manuscript, too. If you or your colleagues have any manuscript or are working on it, please don't hesitate to contact us with detailed synopsis and contents, for its publication. We take utmost care in production and give wide publicity to the book and its author. We can also suggest you the title related to your subject for writing, as we are the publishers who believe more in quality than in quantity.

Strategies
in
Defence and Intelligence

Editor-in-Chief

Lt. Gen. S. Pattabhiraman

PVSM, AVSM, SM, VSM (Retd)

(Former Vice Chief of the Army Staff)

- General Shankar Roy Chowdhury *PVSM, ADC*, (Retd)
- Lt Gen SRR Aiyengar, *PVSM, AVSM, VSM* (Retd)
- Maj Gen YK Gera (Retd)
- Maj Gen Vinod Saighal (Retd)
- Brig Trigunesh Mukherjee, *AVSM* (Retd)
- Brig Vinod Anand (Retd)
- Brig (Dr) H K Kar (Retd)
- Dr. Yogendra Narain, *IAS* (Retd)
- Maloy Krishna Dhar, *IPS* (Retd)
- Dr Shivathanu Pillai, DRDO

Manas Publications

New Delhi-110002 (INDIA)

Manas Publications
(Publishers, Distributors, Importers & Exporters)
4402/5A, Main Ansari Road,
(Opp. HDFC Bank), Darya Ganj,
New Delhi - 110 002 (INDIA)
Ph.: 23260783, 23265523:, 23842660 (R)
Fax: 011-23272766
E-mail: manaspublications@vsnl.com
web site: www.manaspublications.in

2009

ISBN 978-81-7049-336-5
Rs. **495/-**

Typeset at
Manas Publications

Printed in India at
Shakti Printing Press, Delhi
and Published by Mrs Suman Lata for
Manas Publications, 4402/5A, Main Ansari Road,
Opp. HDFC Bank, Darya Ganj,
New Delhi - 110 002 (INDIA)

Preface

Warfare, as is known to have been practiced between antagonists, dates back to the Stone Age. Conventional Warfare in this present information age relies heavily on Electronic Warfare technologies. Information and Intelligence gathering have always played a vital role in any war. The next major war may be a nuclear war where little reaction time is left to either side to respond and to survive. The Revolution in Military Affairs ensures deployment of sophisticated military technologies and their continuous development. Maintenance of National Security including Global Security is of prime importance for every country.

Notable defence analysts and experts have carefully presented their opinions on important issues such as Defence Procurement of India, Pakistan's Intelligence, Preparation for Nuclear Disaster, Network Centric Warfare Operations in air, land and sea and Jungle Warfare.

The authors have suggested precise strategies for maintaining National and Global Security and discussed current developments in various defence technologies. The book provides an invaluable source of reference to military commanders and defence scholars.

Contents

The Contributors

Lt Gen S Pattabhiraman, PVSM, AVSM, SM, VSM (Retd) was the first Director-General of Information Systems and later on served as the Vice Chief of the Army Staff and the Colonel Commandant of the Bombay Sappers.

General Shankar Roy Chowdhury, PVSM, ADC (Retd) is a former Chief of the Army Staff. Post retirement, the General has taken to active politics. As a member of the Rajya Sabha he has highlighted and raised Defence related issues with great passion and vigour in the Parliament.

Dr. Yogendra Narain, IAS (Retd) is a Ph.D. in Public Administration, M.A. in Political Science, B.Sc., Diploma in Development Economics (University of Glasgow). Belongs to the 1965 batch of the Indian Administrative Service (IAS). A Gold Medallist of the Allahabad University, he has had an illustrious career of more than four decades as a civil servant.

He has held various important positions such as Chief Secretary of Uttar Pradesh; Secretary, Ministry of Surface Transport and Defence Secretary, Government of India. In view of his wide experience, he was appointed as the Secretary General of the Rajya Sabha—the Upper House of the Parliament of India—the distinguished post which he held for more than five years.

A keen student of Political Science, he has written several articles on Public Administration on a vide array of topical issues and edited several parliamentary publications.

He believes that Public Administration and Governance should continuously reform itself and innovation should be its inherent characteristic. Towards this end he has made several presentations and experimented with new ideas while setting up the National Highway Authority of India (NHAI) and the Greater Noida Development Authority on the outskirts of Delhi.

Lt Gen SRR Aiyengar, PVSM, AVSM, VSM (Retd) is a former Commandant of National Defence College, New Delhi, Defence Services Staff College, Wellington and the Military College of Telecommunication Engineering, Mhow.

Major General Y K Gera (Retd) was ADG SI and CSO Central Command and Deputy Director and Editor of USI from 01 Jan 1997 to 30 April 2007.

Maj Gen Vinod Saighal (Retd) from the Indian Army in 1995, from the post of Director General of Military Training. Before that he had several active command assignments including the command of an independent armoured formation and mountain and desert divisions. An officer from the cavalry, he had held assignments with UN peackeeping forces as well as tenures in the Middle East. He served as the country's Military Attache in France and Benelux. He has a wide range of interests and speaks several languages including French and Persian. Currently he is the Executive Director of Eco Monitors Society (EMS), a non-governmental organization (NGO) concerned with demography and ecology. After retirement he founded the Movement for Restoration of Good Government (MRGG).

He has several articles on a vast range of subjects to his credit and is the author of the internationally acclaimed books *Restructuring South Asian Security, Restructuring Pakistan, Dealing with Global Terrorism: The Way Forward and Third Millennium Equipoise.*

Brig Trigunesh Mukherjee, AVSM (Retd) is a former faculty member at the College of Defence Management and Army War College. After leaving the army as ADG-NCC, he has been conducting learning programs in the corporate sector. He has developed and led programs in areas of human behaviour like Teamship, Leadership, Creativity, Exploring Potential and Achievement Orientation. Trigunesh has worked with companies like Lufthansa, Motorola, UT Star, E-Funds, Tata Motors and DHL.

Brig. Vinod Anand (Retd) is a Senior Fellow at United Service Institution of India (USI).

Brig (Dr) H K Kar (Retd) was commissioned in the Corps of Engineers (Indian Army) in 1968. He is an alumni of National Defence Academy (Khadakvasla), College of Military Engineering (Pune), Defence Services Staff College (Wellington) and National Defence College (New Delhi).

Participation in the 1971 Indo Pak War, raising an army unit, commanding an engineer regiment in Ladakh, providing engineer support to military stations as Chief Engineer of the Zone, being the engineer advisor to a Strike Corps of the army, are some of the highlights of his career. He has been an instructor in the College of Military Engineering and Army War College (Mhow) and is a recipient of the Chief of Army Staff Commendation Card.

In the field of civil education, he has done PhD in Management, M Tech in Management and Systems, MSc in Defence Studies and Graduation in Mechanical Engineering.

He was Deputy Director General NBC Warfare in the Perspective Planning Directorate, Army Headquarters, heading the apex body of the army in the field of NBC Warfare.

Maloy Krishna Dhar, IPS (Retd) served the Intelligence Bureau, India's prime intelligence agency for nearly three decades, during which he conducted and witnessed innumerable counter-terrorism, counter-espionage and political operations. He specialized in counter-intelligence measures to meet Pakistan's overt and covert aggression and the proxy war it had unleashed against India. He retired as its Joint Director. After retirement he has taken up freelance journalism and professional writing. He has written a number of books, which include two books of fiction *"Operation Triple X: An Indian Spy Run in Pakistan"* and *"Bitter Harvest"*. He also co-authored *"Pakistan After 9/11"*. His recent publications are *"Open Secrets: India's Intelligence Unveiled"* and *"Fulcrum of Evil: ISI-CIA-Al Qaeda Nexus"*.

Dr Shivathanu Pillai, Distinguished Scientist & the architect of BRAHMOS supersonic cruise missile joint venture with Russia, is the Chief Controller, DRDO for Naval systems and CEO & MD of BrahMos Aerospace. He contributed in the development of rocket motors for SLV-3 the first Satellite Launch Vehicle of India, as a core team member of the project at Vikram Sarabhai Space Centre, Thiruvananthapuram. Later, he was Programme Director for Integrated Guided Missile Development Programme at DRDL, Hyderabad where he contributed in the development of critical technologies usng a network of academic institutions, R&D labs and industries which helped raising Agni, Prithvi, Nag, Trishul and Akash missiles. He was also instrumental in development and induction of indigenous underwater sensors and weapon system in Indian Navy.

Dr. Pillai, is the author of many technical papers, and co-author of the book *"Envisioning an Empowered Nation"* with Dr. A.P.J. Abdul Kalam and authored book *"Ocean Warfare:- The Technology Waves"* He is a recipient of various national and international awards including Padmashree and Fellow/ Member of professional societies.

1

Information Warfare Technologies: The Inevitable Future of Strategic Warfare and India

*MAJ GEN YK GERA (RETD)**

Introduction

1. During the last couple of decades, there has been a technological change with the advent of the information revolution. In the words of Cosmos, the character in the motion picture *Sneaker*, 'The world is not run by weapons anymore, or energy or money. It is run by ones and zeroes-little bits of data. It's all electrons ... and there's a war there.'[1] The potential created for different types of warfare in cyberspace seems unlimited.

* Maj Gen YK Gera (Retd) was ADG SI and CSO Central Command

2. Since the 1991 Gulf War, defence planners all over the world have been focusing on Information Warfare and its exploitation to their advantage. Concurrently, the trend is towards acceleration in the pace of digitization of society with exponential growth in the use of the Internet, and an increasing portion of everyday life going online.

3. The 21st Century is witness to unprecedented revolution in the field of Information Technology (IT). Modern means of communication have turned the world into an integrated and seamless network of information. There has been a dramatic increase in use of Personal Computers (PCs), Internet, mobile phones, black berries, iPods, and spread of e-commerce. Business activities are being better coordinated with the setting up of inter-industry data-bases, transcending corporate boundaries and forming the nervous system for the full spectrum of corporate activities by sharing information.

What is Information Warfare?

4. The debate over definition of Information Warfare rages fiercely. At one extreme are the radicals who argue that future wars can be won without bloodshed by achieving 'information dominance'. Sceptics at the other end of the spectrum note that information has always been recognized as a key factor in warfare. They acknowledge that today's techniques and technologies for manipulating information are new, but insist that the battle to control information is only one more field of battle which supports the other three—land, sea, and air.[2]

5. Martin C Libicki has identified seven distinct forms of warfare which involve the protection, manipulation, degradation, and denial of information.[3] These are as follows:-

(a) Command and Control Warfare: strikes against the enemy's head and neck.

(b) Intelligence-based Warfare: comprises design, protection and denial of systems that seek sufficient knowledge to dominate the battle space.

(c) Electronic Warfare: radio, electronic, or cryptographic techniques.

(d) Psychological Warfare: information used to change the minds of friends, neutrals and foes.

(e) Hacker Warfare: in which computer systems are attacked.

(f) Economic Info War: to block and channel information to pursue economic dominance.

(g) Cyber Warfare: a futuristic scenario.

6. Information Warfare may encompass 'actions taken to achieve information superiority by affecting adversary information, information based processes, information systems and computer based networks, while leveraging and defending one's own information'. There has been considerable proliferation in information systems with convergence of computers and telecommunications. Information infrastructures are made of a large number of communication networks interlinked at different levels. The boundaries between civilian, military, and international systems are progressively getting dismantled[4].

Space and IT

7. **Concept of Space as a Force Multiplier**. Space assets have become hub for communications, surveillance, guidance, navigation, and research and development activities. The two Gulf wars and the war in Afghanistan have vindicated the concept of space as a force multiplier for military operations. India is a 'Space Faring Nation' with a potential for harnessing space assets for ground, maritime, and air operations. The architecture for military missions would need 'Net Work Centric Warfare Capability' with pre-positioned configuration of satellites. Proper monitoring would be required for detection and destruction of military targets, using different means.

8. **Different Types of Satellites**. Satellites having relevance to military applications are as under:-

(a) *Surveillance Satellites.* These are used for battle-field surveillance and arms control verification. These act as eyes and ears include: Electronic Reconnaissance Satellites, Photographic Reconnaissance Satellites, and Imagery Satellites.

(b) *Ocean Surveillance Satellites.* These can help in ascertaining height of waves, strength, and direction of ocean currents, detection of submarines, salinity of water and so on.

(c) *Navigation Satellites.* These help in navigation and global positioning. The US *Navstar* Global Positioning System (GPS) is facilitating global services. The Europeans are also producing a *Gallelio* system with international collaboration.

From the year 2008 onwards, India has programmed to launch satellites for Indian Regional Navigational and Positional system.

(d) *Geodetic Satellite.* For studying physical nature of earth and help in producing maps. The pattern of earth's gravitational potential can also be studied.

(e) *Nano-Satellites.* These represent a revolutionary breakthrough in miniaturization and thrust for future satellite development. These satellites will help in increased survivability and flexibility of future space systems.

9. **Anti-Satellite Weapons (ASW)**. Laser based Directed Energy Weapons (DEW) can be used for destroying or damaging a satellite. There would also be a need to develop Anti-Anti Satellite Weapons (AASW). This aspect requires more research. Recently, China tested satellite destruction technique, creating international furore.

10. **Space Assets**. These include military, civil, commercial, and other accessible space systems, their supporting infrastructure including terrestrial elements and personnel who operate them.

11. **Space Systems**. These comprise nodes and links. Space node includes satellites, space stations and reusable space transportable system like space shuttle. Terrestrial nodes include land, sea, and airborne equipment used to interact with space nodes through control and mission links. Control links enable dissemination of mission data. An adversary can target nodes and links to degrade the ability to conduct operations.

12. **Space Weapons**. Space weapons may be banned. However, some nations are already carrying out secret research and trials. These weapons could be based on kinetic or chemical energy. Directed Energy Weapons (DEW) including LASER beams fall in this category.

13. **Network Centric Warfare**. Combat edge will be with forces that are better networked rather than platform based weapon systems. The emerging architecture demands land, sea, air and space based electronic, photographic and sensor equipment to be networked to gather surveillance and intelligence data. These are then passed to data fusion centre integrated with decision making system. Analysis and dissemination is done using automated systems. As and when the Command, Control, Communications, Computers, Intelligence, Inter-operability, Surveillance and Reconnaissance (C4I2SR) systems of the armed forces are fielded, these would get integrated. It would also enhance nuclear deterrence capabilities. C4I2SR cannot operate without fully automated systems.

Cyber Space: New Theatre of War

14. **Cyber Space Definition.**[5] As per the February 2003 US Government document, *The National Strategy to Secure Cyber Space*: "Cyberspace is the nervous system of nation's critical infrastructures and is composed of a large number of interconnected computers, servers, routers, switches and fibre optic cables. A nation's critical infrastructures composed of public and private institutions in the sector of agriculture, food, water, public health, emergency services, government,

defence industrial base, energy, information and finance, chemicals and hazardous materials, postal and shipping". The document emphasizes that securing cyberspace is a difficult strategic challenge that requires co-ordinated and focused effort from the entire society—the federal government, state and local governments, the private sector, and the people.

15. **Space Supremacy**. Till mid 1980s, Space was considered as a new battlefield after land, sea, and air. Emphasis was on developing technologies to build and launch missiles and Satellite Launch Vehicles (SLV), to guard against likely emergence of 'star war' capabilities of advanced countries, and control space for economic benefits.

16. **Information Superiority**. During the 1990s information superiority started becoming more important. Concept of knowledge power and knowledge industry emerged. Indian software engineers contributed substantially to the US and other advanced countries becoming information giants. The race is on and has added a fifth dimension to ground, sea, air and space as a theatre for war.

17. **Information Technology and Cyber Warfare**. Information Technology is a double edged weapon. While providing opportunities, it introduces new vulnerabilities and threats pertaining to hardware, software, skinware, and network connectivity. Information dominance is essential. Information Technology non-lethal weapons can destroy valuable data, black out communication networks and cripple the nation. Cyber warfare can be a full fledged war with national infrastructure as target. For conduct of cyber warfare national level decision making would be required in real time. For such operations, good monitoring of network traffic, web sites, and data bases; intrusion detection; encryption and decryption and remote access facilities would be required. Cyber warfare weapons have range of Inter-Continental Ballistic Missiles (ICBM) and speed of high power LASER and lethality of both. It is not possible to limit their battle space, because they are

borderless. Information Warfare is the warfare of the 21st Century wherein disruption of an enemy's vital information infrastruçture would prove more disastrous than the physical destruction of a vital asset. To take an example, in India jeopardizing the communication infrastructure of the Software Technology Parks engaged in software and IT exports, would have serious financial implications. In China, People's Liberation Army conducted a network exercise by simulating cyber attacks on telecommunications, banking and finance, power and energy grids, and selected defence networks of Taiwan, India, and South Korea[6] with a reasonable degree of success. The Chinese information Warfare doctrine includes 'doctoring' of chips and software that can plant viruses and 'trap- doors' in enemy's information systems[7]. This is a cause for concern because in India we have a thriving piracy market and software CDs from China are available at low prices.

INDIA AND STRATEGIC WARFARE

Historical Background

18. Historically India has been a rich country. There has been a flow of invaders, adventurers and traders to seek fortune in India. Invaders from Central Asia seized power in North India and established empires with ease. Besides factors like lack of unity among Indian kingdoms, absence of a common threat perception and a combined response, a point which needs highlighting is the 'technology difference' between large native forces and small foreign forces in terms of firepower and speed. Simply put, it was a charge of the invading light horse mounted cavalry brigades inflicting heavy damage on the elephant mounted Indian forces. Later introduction of rifle into the armed forces by invaders resulted in combat edge of vast proportions. Similarly use of canons by Babur in the battle of Panipat led to victory by the invading forces. Battlefield advantages in favour of the invading forces led to victories, and in due course, to "regime changes" imposed by the victorious. High speed of attack, superior manoeuvrability and weapon

delivery with precision, significantly altered the politico-military-social landscape of India.

19. A study of the history of establishment of British rule in India also has a common thread in terms of "technology difference." Representatives of 'East India Company' came to India and secured "concessions" from the ruling elites, initially on the coasts for transacting commerce. They were also permitted after suspicious negotiations a small force for protection of trading interests. That, these small forces came with contemporary weapon systems was imprecisely appreciated and understood. Technological differential facilitated achievement of their goal resulted in India being enslaved by the British.

20. India attained independence in 1947 and substantial development and progress has been taking place during the last six decades. All round development have been coming in political, economic, judicial and social reforms. And they have been implemented with varying degree of success. The Indian economy is doing well. India's search for major power status is being pursued even as progress in the important fields of poverty removal, population control, health, and education sectors continues to be tardy.

India—An Emerging Power

21. The 21st Century is being viewed as one in which new powers will emerge on the international scene. India figures in every list as the new emerging power. Many believe, this would serve as a stabilizing element, while some view its potential power as a countervailing element in the emerging world order. For India, to play a meaningful role in the global power structure, there is a need for clarity on its strategic perspectives and priorities. To do this interdependent matrix, incorporating all elements of the national strategic necessity will have to be worked out. Strategy depends on combination of economic strength and resilience, vibrant political institutions that anticipate and deal with challenges, a readiness to sacrifice for larger

causes, and finally credible military power. These instruments need to be well coordinated and optimized for attaining national objectives.

India—Potentially a Future IT Superpower

22. The turn of the century led the western nations to seek solution to Y2K problems. The Indian software industry helped them and earned $ 2.5 b during the period 1996-1999. Ever since, the Indian software industry has been growing at a fast pace. Some indicators[8] are as under:-

(a) For the past five years or so the Indian IT industry is averaging a compounded annual growth rate of 40.5 per cent. During 2005, the industry earned $ 8.6 b.

(b) During 2005-2006, software exports amounted to $ 4 b, accounting for 20.5 per cent of India's total exports.

(c) The highest certification a software company can achieve is Capability Maturity Model-5 (CMM-5). In the world there are 23 software companies having such competence with Carnegie Melton Software Engineering Institute (SEI). Of these 16 are Indian.

(d) Of the 500 Fortune Companies, 185 outsourced their software requirements to India in 2005-2006.

23. A Regional Cyber Security and Research Centre (RCSRC) was opened at Chandigarh in April 2007. The Centre is to engage a multidisciplinary team of researchers and faculty to conduct specialist research in areas of cyber and information security, and performance optimization in networking in a cost effective manner. The mission is to encourage, promote, facilitate, and execute research in areas related to the nexus of society and the internet.

24. The Indian Government has recognized the potential of IT as a vehicle for progress and for leveraging India to an IT superpower status. Accordingly, the National Task

Force for IT and Software Development has worked out a roadmap for the Indian IT Industry.

India's Strategic Culture

25. As per Ken Booth a British scholar, the concept of strategic culture refers to a nation's traditions, values, attitudes, patterns of behaviour, habits, symbols, achievements and particular ways of adapting to the environment and solving problems with respect to the threat and use of force[9]. However, these factors indicate trends and not a finite state of affairs. Some strategic thinkers blame India for lack of strategic culture. This is probably true if we analyse India's past history. However, things seem to be changing for the better since independence in 1947. This period of six decades or so upto 2007 can be divided into four phases, broadly corresponding to the periods in which India's foreign policy adapted to meet threats to Indian strategic interests. These are the Non-Aligned Movement phase from 1947 to 1962, the bipolar phase from 1963 to 1970, the military diplomacy phase from 1971 to 1990, and the post Cold War phase from 1991 to 2007. India has adapted to the international strategic environment with skill, though at a slow pace. Things seem to be improving. However, Indian Government's apparent lack of 'will' due to internal pressures could be an impediment.

Emerging Ingrediants of Strategic Warfare

26. **Security Environment**. The 21st Century security environment is rapidly moving away from that of the previous century. The 20th Century belief in the territorial determinants of strategy and security is no longer relevant. A system that is divided between the traditional 20th Century state-centred model and the 21st Century substate and trans-state model is taking shape. Security threats are more likely to be directed against societies instead of the armed forces across the borders. The process of globalization in human resource management, economic development, technological

development, and asymmetrical warfare has considerably transformed the strategic scene. Strategies for homeland security and defence of national boundaries are intimately linked. The threats of asymmetric warfare through attacks on infrastructure, economic targets, societal cohesion and national leadership have led to adoption of hard measures even by democratic states.

27. **Militarisation and Weaponisation of Space.** Militarisation of space falls within the definition of utilizing the services of satellites for enhancing performance of terrestrially based weapons, surveillance, and communication systems. Weaponisation involves placing of weapon systems in space i.e. using space platforms. Deployment of Anti-Ballistic Missile (ABM) measures may find place in space. However, the current outer space treaty prohibits weaponisation. Despite this, some nations are carrying out secret research and trials.

Inevitability of Enhanced use of Information Warfare Technology during Future Strategic Warfare

28. For conduct of military operations there are three fundamentals—principles of war, strategy of war fighting, and technology. While the principles of war and strategy have evolved at a slow pace, technology for war fighting has been growing at a revolutionary pace. There has been a rapid development in technology with information technology at the core. Main aspects are as under:-

(a) Precision guided munitions covering long distances are becoming main form of combat. Their use during the 2001 Afghan War and 2003 Iraq War has been very effective. Modern weapon systems use digital mode and are very responsive.

(b) The trend is towards downsizing of combat forces. It involves reducing numbers, readjusting force structures, and optimizing combat and logistic elements. The emphasis is on achieving stronger combat capabilities while reducing the size of military forces.

(c) For effective command and control, automation is being resorted to progressively. Commencing with C^3I system, military automation systems of most major countries have progressed to C4I2 and C4I2SR (Command, Control, Communications, Computers, Intelligence, Inter-operability, Surveillance, and Reconnaissance System). These systems facilitate real time, efficient, command and control capabilities.

(d) From the traditional land, sea, and air forces, expansion is taking place in two more dimensions to include space and electromagnetic spectrum. Armed forces with knowledge based superior capabilities to control flow of information are bound to dominate high technology future battlefield. Security of own information structure and the ability to disrupt that of the adversary will be a reasonably good capability indicator.

(e) Jointmanship and integration of space based capability must be viewed holistically. Integration of land, sea, air, and space inclusive of precision guided munitions covering intercontinental ranges with fully automated and secure command and control set up need to be evolved expeditiously. Combat edge will be with the forces that are better networked rather than those having better platform weapons.

Conclusion

29. The telecommunication revolution brought in the death of 'distance'. Satellite broadcasting led to the concept of 'global village'. Cyber space has introduced a phrase 'Universal Desktop'. The world is at our finger tips. We just have to click and open windows to the universe. It is reasonable to anticipate our accelerating transition to a knowledge based society in the light of leapfrogging strides in infrastructure development and networking.

30. India has earned a significant place in the global IT industry and aspires to be an IT superpower in the future. With an expanding IT infrastructure, the nation is getting connected to the 'global village' at a rapid pace. Ironically, the technology that empowers us, also exposes us to new threats. These threats do not recognize borders and impinge on nearly every cross-section of our society. The threat is not only to the government or the military, but also to the private industry and the entire society at large. In such a scenario, it is imperative to work out strategies to maximize the opportunities provided by connectivity while minimizing the associated risks.

31. We should learn from our history and not allow 'technological difference' to seep into our system to our disadvantage. God has bestowed us with good brain power as a nation. The global powers have just graduated to the 'knowledge world' phase and IT industry is booming. India has carved out its place in the prevailing scenario. All emerging indicators point towards inevitability of enhanced use of Information Warfare Technology during future strategic warfare. We must continue to strive hard not only to keep abreast but also enhance our operational capabilities and retain leadership role.

References

1. Krishnan, Murali and Ashutosh Kumar Sinha. 'Spider on the Web', *Outlook*, pp.16-8. 15 March 1999.
2. Laquer, Walter. 1996. 'Postmodern Terrorism', *Foreign Affairs*, September/ October, p 24.
3. Rathmell, A. 1997. "Çyber-Terrorism: The shape of Future Conflict', *RUSI Journal*, p. 40. October.
4. Gera, Y. K. 1999. 'Cyber Terrorism: The Newest Face of Terror', *Aakrosh* 2 (3); April.
5. Sandlas, Ved Prakash. 2006 'Çyber-Space Security.' *U.S.I. Journal* Vol cxxxvi, No, 565 (July- September 2006).

6. Prasad R.V. 'Hack the Hackers', *The Hindustan Times*, 19 December 2000.

7. Anand A. Lt Cdr. *Information Technology: The Future Warfare Weapon*, Ocean Books Pvt Ltd, New Delhi, p56.

8. www.mit.gov.in

9. Ken Booth, The Concept of Strategic Culture Affirmed, C. Jacobsen(ed), *Strategic Power: USA/USSR*, Macmillan, London, 1990.

* * *

2

National Security and Higher Defence in India—A Revisit

*GENERAL SHANKAR ROY CHOWDHURY PVSM, ADC, (RETD)**

The Kargil Border War between India and Pakistan took place in May 1999, almost exactly a year after, both the countries had attained nuclear/declared nuclear weapon status following their explosions of devices at Pokaran/Chagai respectively. Though Kargil was a comparatively limited conflict – a single battle really - restricted to one sector of the Line of Control in Kashmir, it nevertheless became a watershed event in the Indian national psyche through the vivid and extensive media coverage which impacted massively on the public consciousness, which in time has generated fundamental and far reaching effects on perceptions of national security both within and outside the government. Patriotic sentiment on Kargil rose to

* General Shankar Roy Chowdhury PVSM, ADC, (Retd) was Chief of the Army Staff, Indian Army.

unprecedented heights, and was perhaps amongst the important considerations which impelled the Government of the time (undoubtedly in an election mode) to establish the Subramaniam Committee immediately after the termination of the conflict, with the charter of analyzing the Kargil War and presenting its report to the Parliament. The Committee commenced its task on 29 July 1999 and tabled its report on 23 February 2000, which was further examined by a Group of Ministers (GoM), who submitted their own recommendations in February 2001 (fairly expeditious by accepted Indian rates of progress!), instituting changes in the system for management of higher defence and national security. The proposed Indian model was essentially a roll-on version of the almost universal American pattern, itself derived from the British system evolved in the 1920's, created by re-engineering the earlier system, from where many basic components had been carried over unchanged, with modifications and add-ons, where necessary. However, due to pressures from political and military vested interests, implementation of the Subramaniam Committee Report has been selective and cosmetic including on some of the most important and significant issues. In the context of the Report, it must also not be forgotten that integrated management of national security and higher defence is not something of recent origin in India. A model and methodology considered appropriate for its time was established almost concurrently with Independence, under the guidance of Lord Ismay, the Chief of Staff to Lord Mountbatten, the last British Viceroy and the first Governor General of the country. It was a collegiate system based on a network of committees which worked by consultation and consensus – the Defence Committee of the Cabinet at the apex supported by a Defence Minister's Committee at Ministry level, and the Chiefs of Staff Committee at Joint Services level, the latter with its own subsidiary infrastructure of inter–service committees at working level, such as the Joint Planning Committee and others. Lower down the chain, at theatre and formation level of the land and air forces was the system of army – air coordination established during the Second World War was retained, unchanged in the form of detachments from the regional air forces co-located with army command and corps headquarters (Advanced Headquarters Air Force with its Command Headquarters, and Tactical Air Centres – TAC - with each Corps Headquarters). As an entity, the Committee system is as good as any other, always provided that the political and organizational culture and discipline exists to make it work, without which the most ideal system would become non–functional. Ismay's model functioned effectively enough in planning and directing India's wars immediately post-Independence, handling the First Kashmir War and the Hyderabad Operations of 1947–48. These were adhoc campaigns conducted on shoestring resources, but handling these challenges firmly grounded the fledging Indian planning staff to stand on its own. However, within a decade or so, in the late 1950s and 60s, the system started unravelling, essentially due to prolonged neglect by the Prime Minister of all military matters magnified by an abrasive internal environment within the Services created by Defence Minister (cum "political commissar") VK Krishna Menon, who displayed all the symptoms of an unstable "loose cannon". Though the causes were mainly politico–bureaucratic, the military contributed their own share to the process of devaluation, with increased jostling and elbowing between the three Services, often accompanied by inter-personal frictions at high level, primarily for allocation of share in meager defence budgets, attempts at inter–Services one-upmanship by playing up to the political and bureaucratic establishments, and conflicting perceptions of each service on various major and minor professional issues of common concern. As governmental concern and attention towards defence and national security spiraled steadily downwards in the late 1950's and 60's, inputs by the military hierarchy on issues of national security were increasingly disregarded, if not totally ignored as superfluous or irrelevant, and the role of inter-Services planning was gravely diminished.

Against this backdrop, Operation Vijay for the liberation of the Portuguese colonies in India, - Goa, Daman and Diu– was launched in 1961. This tri-service mini–operation was in effect little more than a training exercise with a live enemy (almost like the German invasion of Poland in 1939), but even this relatively minor effort flashed warning signs of organizational dysfunction within the system. These were ignored in the larger political euphoria over the low–cost victory, but alas, the next round was just around the corner. This came about in 1962, but this time against an immeasurably stronger opponent – the People's Liberation Army of China. The scene was Tibet, and the wages of sustained neglect were - defeat.

While Pakistan established itself as India's permanent security problem right from the initial stage of creation of both countries in August 1947, the People's Republic of China, emerged in 1950 as another and far more serious challenge after, when the People's Liberation Army (PLA) entered Tibet and the Sino–Indian boundary, traditionally quiescent was activated. The Sino–Indian boundary issue carried large historical baggage, and both parties had their own perceptions which certainly merited dispassionate examination and discussions, but it was gradually apparent that softer options of dialogue and diplomacy had failed to resolve the outstanding issues. Attitudes gradually hardened on both sides until the possibility of a military confrontation between the two countries could not be regarded as unthinkable. For India, the entire period of almost a decade over which the Sino–Indian border fermented, the developing situation had warranted close and focused synergies between the military, diplomatic, and political establishments, and, even more importantly, between the three wings of the Armed Forces themselves, but this had not been forthcoming. Rather, an environment of political complacency and fevered optimism in Panchsheel had been generated within the government, and no pro–active contingency planning had been allowed in the context of possible hostilities with China. The Defence Committee of the Cabinet, the apex organization for strategic decision making, had become a highly personalized caucus under the personal direction of the Prime Minister, "advised" (if one can use the term) by an inner group composed, not of ministerial colleagues or the professional military hierarchy as might have been expected, but an assortment of individuals who enjoyed his personal trust and confidence. Notable members of this "club" were the irascible VK Krishna Menon, a Defence Minister who refused to hear any evil about China; Lt Gen BM Kaul, the Chief of General Staff (CGS), a pushy upwardly mobile aspirant with sketchy military credentials but Nehruvian connections, and Mr BN Mullick, the shadowy Director of the Intelligence Bureau, considered as Jawaharlal Nehru's de facto National Security Adviser, decades before the term came into vogue, who cultivated an aura of omnipotence and omniscience - but was to prove disastrously inept in handling his professional responsibility of providing even approximately adequate intelligence based on which appropriate policies and responses could be evolved at national level. The Indian Army at the time was in no state to undertake any serious operations against a power which had intervened in the Korean War and fought the United States to a standstill. The Nehruvian regime had always downplayed the military, and, as a result, the Indian Army and Air Force which would be involved to the maximum in such an eventuality, (the Indian Navy perhaps less so) had both become severely impoverished by prolonged neglect. In addition the Army had also been extensively diverted on construction of its own accommodation on Operation Amar, laudable enough, but detracting greatly from operational preparedness. Besides being deployed piecemeal in militarily unsound and untenable locations all along the Sino–Indian border in support of Operation Onkar (1959 -62), the brain child of BN Mullick, a "forward policy" of confrontation with the People's Republic of China on the border issue by establishing a string of police detachments without any tactical considerations, and with an almost child–like disregard for possible consequences. Professional inputs and advice by

Indian military commanders like Lt General SPP Thorat calling for restraint and limited forward deployment until adequate military build up could be achieved were considered unpalatable and hence rejected. There was no credible intelligence on Chinese military capabilities and intentions, but grossly optimistic inputs from the Intelligence Bureau regarding the strength and likely reactions of Chinese forces in Tibet, encouraged Jawaharlal Nehru to disregard military advice. Events came to a boil throughout 1960–61 culminating in India–China Border War of October–November 1962 even as Jawaharlal Nehru breezily announced his decision for war to a press audience as he took off for the United Nations after premptorily ordering the Army to "throw the Chinese out". Easier said than done, Chinese armies of hitherto undetermined strength and intentions, emerged out of Tibet to unilaterally secure the Aksaichin in the Ladakh region, until halted by stout resistance at Chushul, while India suffered severe military defeats in the Kameng and Lohit regions of the North East Frontier agency (NEFA) at Sela – Bomdila and Walong respectively. The continuous neglect and procedural short circuiting of the whole process for strategic planning and higher direction of war exacted a heavy price. Apart from deploying an Army ill-equipped and unprepared, the political "core committee" vetoed the employment of Indian airpower in an offensive role against the Chinese ground forces without ever consulting the Chiefs of Staff Committee or the Indian Air Force. Indeed, in the context of "higher direction of war" in 1962, the causes of India's military reverses rested totally with the upper echelons of the Government and its politico–bureaucratic establishment and senior military command. The long list of omissions included the prolonged neglect of the Armed Forces under the Nehruvian dispensation, a fractured politico–military interface and resultant aberrations in decision making, intense friction and mistrust engineered by the abrasive Defence Minister VK Krishna Menon, ineffective inter–Service operational planning and coordination, incorrect decisions by senior military commanders, and finally the astonishingly flawed intelligence assessments by the Director of Intelligence Bureau regarding the entire Sino–Indian situation and the many politico–military missteps which resulted from it. 1962 was indeed the darkest hour for the Indian armed forces, but let the record stand that wherever the Indian soldier was lead from the front by his officers, he fought to the death even in the most adverse of circumstances. At higher echelons, General PN Thapar tendered his resignation entirely in the best traditions of the Service, but by sharp contrast Defence Minister Krishna Menon hung on to his office, until driven out by a loud public outcry which forced the hands of the Prime Minister. But as always, every single bureaucrat escaped unscathed – upholding the best traditions of the bureaucracy!

The reverses of 1962 certainly administered major shock therapy to the Indian defence mechanism, and generated intense introspection within and outside the military. On the military side, senior commanders realized the necessity of not succumbing to political or other extraneous pressures or cajolery, into complying with unsound mandates from politico–bureaucratic incumbents. On the political side, matters were more amorphous, and popular outrage, reflected through the Parliament, forced a change of political leadership. Confronted with the harsh reality of numerous organizational lacunae and shortcomings within the system, the higher echelons of national leadership perhaps realized to some extent the value of professional military advice and positive relationships with its hierarchy. The original cabinet system of politico – military decision making by collegiate consensus was repaired and revived, and functioned reasonably enough though with some inevitable systemic hiccoughs, under a different Prime Minister, Lal Bahadur Shastri and Defence Minister Yashwant Rao Chavan in the next war which followed a bare three years later in 1965, this time with Pakistan. The Indo–Pakistan War of 1971 merits a special mention because the establishment of Bangladesh as a viable independent nation was the successful outcome of dynamic politico–diplomatic strategy, backed by a determined military campaign, the whole directed and focussed with determination by a dynamic Prime Minister, Srimati Indira Gandhi, provides a rare historic example of a clear politico–military victory achieved even with a so–called traditional system of strategic management, and confirms what is obvious – any system is only as good or as ineffective as the people operating it. The system which collapsed so disastrously in 1962 under a particular leadership, totally vindicated itself under a different circumstances in 1971, so looking back in retrospect from the first decade of the Twenty First Century, the Nehru – Menon – Mullick phenomena of 1962 can be regarded as an extreme historical aberration generated by the coincidental combination of a particular set of political personalities at that particular period of time. And not really manifested since in any of the subsequent wars, the Indian armed forces participated in the two "full fledged" Indo-Pakistan wars in 1965 and 1971, (after both of which the other two services commented about the overbearing attitude of the Army Chiefs!), a limited but intense "border war" at Kargil in 1999 and a coercive forward concentration in 2001 (Operation Parakram) following the attack on the Indian Parliament in 2001), two significant regional support missions in Sri Lanka (Operation Pawan 1987 – 1989/90) and the Maldives (Operation Cactus 1988) plus extended internal security operations in Punjab, Jammu and Kashmir and the North East against Pakistan–sponsored low intensity war which remains ongoing; and combatised United Nations deployments in Congo, Cambodia, Somalia, Angola, Lebanon and other assorted hot spots.

After Pokaran 1998, India added the nuclear dimension to its strategic capabilities, almost a decade after Pakistan was estimated to have done so clandestinely, assisted by Chinese proliferation. Following the Indian explosions, Pakistan followed suit immediately thereafter at Chagai, and publicly demonstrated its own capabilities which had hitherto been kept clandestine. Both countries were now demonstrably nuclear weapon powers, with the Pakistan Army fully in charge of all nuclear weapon systems and facilities, while on the Indian side, control vested totally with the political leadership. Under these circumstances, it was not surprising that the Indian military hierarchy was not associated with the Government formulation of nuclear policy, or its enunciation as "Minimum Deterrence with No First Use" together with a unilateral moratorium on further testing. The nuclear demonstrations of 1998 by both adversaries have added a far sharper edge to their rivalries and focused world attention on the region.

The GoM made several seminal recommendations, as a result of which the Chief of Integrated Defence Staff was formally appointed on 1 October 2001, and the Integrated Defence Staff sanctioned on 23 November the same year. It was thus that the Integrated Defence Staff for the Indian Armed Forces assumed an official existence, a step long debated but never implemented till that time. Appointment of a Chief of Defence Staff to integrate the working of the three Services was in a sense almost the crux of the entire reform process, but vehement opposition from one Service along with intense political lobbying by its former senior officers – a most disturbing manifestation of inter-Service one-upmanship – finally forced this proposal to tread water. The apparent lapse of this institutional headpiece designed to be central to the whole perception of inter-Services integration, is an anomaly (a "headless chicken" which has acquired currency recently!) which makes the Indian system different from the normal pattern elsewhere, perfectly acceptable if accompanied by a considered and logical rationale, and not, as it appears to be the case, by total happenstance. To begin with, the working levels of Government had been none too comfortable with the idea of some kind of a military Supremo, whom some felt might be a potential Frankenstein and even worse still, might demand an enhanced rating in the order of precedence. So there was not too much concern in the Government when the Defence Services succeeded in checkmating themselves by a deadlock on the issue leading to a politico–administrative hiatus which could be reasonably ascribed by the Government to differences amongst the Services themselves. Amongst the additional features of the new system, is the appointment of a National Security Adviser on the American pattern at the apex level, supported by a National Security Advisory Board. Integration of the Ministry of Defence (MoD) and Service Headquarters in a holistic manner which the Report recommended and no doubt intended, is yet another critical recommendation mangled by pressure from bureaucratic lobbies, and manipulated in a cleverly cosmetic fashion by the simplistic subterfuge of redesignating the existing Service headquarters as "integral offices" of the Ministry of Defence (instead of "attached offices" as under the earlier dispensation). Instead of this devious parody, what was in fact required was appropriate restructuring of the existing framework to integrate the military and civil services along with necessary amendments to the official Rules of Business, to make the integrated system functional, by modifying working procedures within the Government to combine military and civil inputs at the working level. The Chiefs of Staff Committee troika have acquired a much enhanced support base in the new Integrated Defence Staff under the Chief of Integrated Staff ("CIS") which has subsumed into its own organization the earlier network of joint inter-services committees. For the present therefore, a hybrid system of tri–Service integration appears to have emerged by default, linking the traditional Chiefs of Staff Committee with a fairly heavyweight Integrated Defence Staff, but without a Chief of Defence Staff! It is a typical compromise in the best Indian tradition, but in the process may well have thrown up a potentially functional model suited to the native genius and environment (the other such example being the so–called "Civil/Military Unified Headquarters" in the context of low–intensity warfare). The feasibility of compensating for the organizational imbalance created by the void of the Chief of Defence Staff requires to be examined – but one possible model that suggests itself could be restructuring the Integrated Defence Staff into a

Joint Services Headquarters under the Chiefs of Staff Committee for integrated planning and implementation of inter–Services decisions.

At the next level below, two integrated tri–service commands were established-Andamans and Nicobar Command and the Strategic Forces Command for control and employment of India's strategic assets, acquired just the previous year. The former is of course an upgradation of the earlier FORTRAN, or Fortress Andamans an inter - Service organization under the Eastern Naval Command, a somewhat anomalous situation now rectified by according it Command status responsible directly to the Chiefs of Staff Committee. The Strategic Forces Command (as well as the proposed Aero–Space Command when established) must also have an inter–Service composition, and a chain of command responsible to the Chiefs of Staff Committee. The earlier plan to place it directly under the proposed Chief of Defence Staff was organizationally illogical, a folly prompted no doubt by traditional politico–bureaucratic apprehensions about the Armed Forces! In fact regional Theatre Commands (or Military Regions in the parlance of some militaries) synergising regional land forces, airpower, and maritime resources under a single integrated multi-service headquarters indicate the way forward towards true interservice integration. This will require a fresh look at the map of India to determine revised locations, operational responsibilities, and geographical boundaries all of which would require very detailed assessments, but keeping in view India's long coastline, island territories. Extended Economic Zone (EEZ) and off shore maritime assets, it would not be out of place here to suggest a Peninsular Theatre integrating air, naval as well as military assets covering the maritime regions on both coastlines.

In conclusion, it is always well to remember that whatever the modality of functioning, it is always desirable if decisions are taken by consensus, though the converse also holds good, that arriving at one depends on the individual personalities involved. It must also be understood that integration is ultimately a state of mind, more than mere organizational or procedural formats. "Jointmanship", a phonetically somewhat unwieldy term, comes from inter-Service familiarization and involves some merger of individual identity and interests for collective benefits, something which may not come very easily or naturally to entities like the Services, with very strong collective bonding and intense corporate loyalties not seen in almost any other profession. In fact may not even be prudent to seriously downplay this aspect, without running the risk of diminishing the unique characteristics which separate the Armed Forces from "the rest". It is also undoubtedly ironic that inter-Service differences occur mostly in peacetime, over long term policy issues, while during war, operational urgencies are resolved fairly expeditiously at all levels including the highest. Service interests are important, and personality differences may exist in some cases, but the troika of Service Chiefs function in harmony and overall inter-personal relationships between the three services are positive, cooperative and warm. For the present, some but not all the building blocks of higher defence organization in India have been emplaced, but though the infrastructure has begun to develop, the system is still far from holistically established, and there seem to be enough variations from established patterns, to raise questions as to whether these resulted from considered decisions taken after deliberate analysis and review, or adhoc adjustments to accommodate extraneous factors.

***

3

Revolution in Military Affairs (RMA)

Lt. Gen. S. Pattabhiraman
*PVSM, AVSM, SM, VSM (Retd)**

Introduction

1. A common military jargon called RMA has been in prolific use during a decade or so, so much so that any technological breakthrough leading to a semblance of a victory in a battle or a conflict is attributed to RMA, amongst other factors.

2. While the recognition of RMA as a battle winning factor is no doubt contributing to enhance use of technology primarily in militaries of the world, there may be a need to sift these RMAs that have had a telling effect in order for a discerning military analyst to observe characteristics of such breakthroughs and their long term effects.

* Lt. Gen. S. Pattabhiraman PVSM, AVSM, SM, VSM (Retd) has been the Vice Chief of the Army Staff, Indian Army.

3. An attempt is being made to make the reader to understand RMAs in correct context, through this journey.

Historical Perspective

4. Warfare as is known to have been practised between antagonists, dates back to stone age, when pieces of stone were used to good effect by primeval man either simply as stone for its weight and velocity or shaped into pointed missiles for greater effect. These could be the earliest RMAs that could have turned the tide of an outcome or a contest by use of force.

5. Battle of Cannae 223 BC when Hannibal cleverly out manoeuvered the Romans by swift movement on foot by large bodies of men and thus trapping the static Roman hordes, was a revolution in tactics and not so much in technology.

6. Progressive use of bows and arrows, spears, swords and shields followed by use of horsed cavalry to devastating effect during revolutions, the latter made famous by Chengis Khan's hordes from Mongolia and Alexander the great, across Persia.

7. The next revolution was the discovery of gunpowder and its use in firearms commencing with the self-loading musket and greater and more powerful use in rifles and cannons. Use of cannons and explosives in particular led to different forms of warfare both offensive and defensive that led to encampments, Forts, Siege warfare and so on.

8. Introduction of Tanks in early 20th century, followed by use of airpower were major thresholds that changed the form of warfare and in its wake caused enormous casualities. Prior to this, from 16th century onwards, use of large warships on seas for transporting men and material and for

escorting them; led to major Naval engagements between sea-faring nations, particularly the European powers. The American civil war itself, besides being a watershed in changing fundamentally the way in which societies are to be organized in future, also revolutionized warfare in structuring Armies into various constituents such as cavalry, gunners, signals and so on.

9. World Wars I and II brought in revolutions, the first in use of tanks and airpower and the second in use of large mechanized forces, as also airborne assaults and towards the end the use of nuclear power to end conflicts. The use of rockets V-1 and V-2 by the Germans gave rise to missile technology and to guided bombs. Blitzkrieg, as a form of ferocious employment of large bodies of mechanized troops over day and night with coordinated use of airpower to paralyse the enemy as practised by Guderian was a major RMA of mid 20th century surpassed only by the development of nuclear weapons.

10. In between, use of Radars was a quiet but effective technological innovation, which in its usage initially in defensive mode but later for both offensive and defensive uses, can claim to have altered the contours of a modern war.

11. The use of electro magnetic spectrum subsequently has led to information warfare, as a major RMA that with use of satellites is likely to be a major force multiplier for decades to come.

Technologies and Revolution

12. Having had an oversight historically on the import of revolutionary changes in warfare, it would be interesting to see the part played by technology and its evolution in significantly altering the course of conflicts by such revolutionary innovations.

13. No doubt, the earliest of the RMAs which transformed fighting was the discovery of gunpowder refined into use of explosives, be it for propelling bullets or for use in bombs and shells. The preponderance in the use of explosives in firearms and in projectiles by Europeans against natives of other continents led to the large-scale colonization of such states by European powers from the 16th to 19th century. This revolution remained unsurpassed until the advent of Tanks and Combat Aircrafts towards the end of World War I, except for the tremendous strides being made on the High Seas with faster and more weaponised ships and crafts being added to the Armada of colonial powers. This revolution caused by the sea-faring powers in turn led to establishment of continental supremacy within Europe signified by Napoleonic, Prussian, Hungarian influences as also on the American civil war across the Atlantic.

14. The coming of the industrial age in 19th century truly heralded major revolutionary changes giving militaries of the superior technological powers, the option of decisive conclusion of a campaign of wars should diplomacy fail, as signified by Earl von Clausewitz's famous maxim.

15. The period between the two World Wars witnessed unprecedented conventional arms production and development of technologies in land, sea and air systems notably in greater lethality and destructive power, development of Radars & Sonars, development of submarines, greater reach of air power over seas in the form of aircraft carriers and proliferation of rocket technology.

16. The end of the Second World War and the commencement of the cold war between capitalist USA led Western Consortium and USSR led communist regimes significantly revolutionized

warfare in three major areas viz., long range and precision missiles both conventional and nuclear, outer space exploitation and stealth technology.

17. End of cold war, break-up of Soviet Union followed by USA's domination and coming into being of a unipolar world has seen great strides being made in unarmed combat with UAV's, UCAV's and robotic control over weapon systems. This has been largely facilitated by the Information-Communication-Technology, called the ICT revolution and phenomenal use of bandwidth, which has given rise to the latest technological and systemic revolution in net centric warfare.

Geo-Political impact on Technology/Warfare changes and civilization/Governmental Transformations

18. A scan of major societal transformations over the years, that have taken place including clash of religions, could be attributed to amongst other factors to RMAs of that period.

19. The war of Crusades effected the logistics of movement of large bodies of horse-based cavalry. The revolution in seafaring ability gave rise to domination by Spanish Armada followed by Nelson's Flotilla and led to colonization of the under-developed continents.

20. Major technological revolutions in Air Power, Rockets & Missiles, precision guided munitions (PGMs) and nuclear power of 20th century has transformed the world into nation states governed by like minded ideologies and protecting their interest and societal values by engaging in forms of military technological practices that suits their budgets and making compromises to keep pace with the requirements of modern warfare.

21. Post German unification, cold-war and break-up of the balance of power between two broadly factions

maintaining status quo in the affairs of the world, the RMA that has come about as a result of unprecedented PGM and non-lethal capability developed and leveraged by USA in particular, western nations in general has brought about break up of nation states such as former Yugoslavia, and formulation of new states such as East Timor and Kosovo.

Asymmetry and Balance

22. Ironically while RMAs have contributed significantly in enhancing capabilities both offensive and defensive of the Armies and nation states that have propagated and conceptualized the practice of the same, telling effect in conventional conflict situations these have however had little or much less than cost effectiveness when pitted against adversaries or movements who have fought for certain causes though placed in an asymmetric manner. The American withdrawal from Vietnam and the Russian defeat in Afghanistan are classical examples of the truism.

23. The first half of the 20th century witnessed a balance between forces each trying to attain conventional superiority in technological and numerical spheres with no significant or decided advantage until the overwhelming power of the atom bomb was used to terminate what seemed an impasse after nearly two long wars interjected by an uneasy peace.

24. The cold war that followed witnessed phenomenal revolutions in missiles, air defence weapons, ISR capabilities, precision engagements and so on and was matched on either side by USSR and USA fielding super high tech weapons and with their proxies testing them selectively. However a balance of mutual destruction was in place. Post break-up

of USSR and re-unification of Germany, USA with its tremendous economic advantage and wealth of knowledge soon overtook the rest of the world in an unprecedented manner. Whether in fielding the Army developed Internet or Global Positioning System (GPS) or in production of very high quality and efficient means of transportation, USA continued to forge ahead of Europe and Russia.

25. Western Europe mainly spearheaded by NATO with recently inducted former eastern block members has now found it justified to use its RMAs to their advantage while deploying its member state's armed forces to Iraq and Afghanistan where again while the asymmetry in military sophisticated technology between warring factions and NATO is striking. However sub conventional nature of insurgency conflicts with use of IEDs, antitank stand-off rockets and use of suicide bombers have largely nullified the technological superiority.

Essentials, Desirables and Wish List

26. Every nation state as constituted today with legitimate sovereign rights to protect its territorial integrity and values, it wishes to uphold, needs to have a viable security structure and therefore a modern military. In order to keep pace with rapid obsolescence of technologies and to be current with RMAs, the state needs to invest what it can offer to stay abreast.

27. Essential RMAs mainly defensive in nature, cover basic armaments i.e. small arms, destroyers/frigates, aircrafts and standard munitions with reasonable night fighting capabilities. Antitank capability and air defence weapons are also essential for a modern army. Unless the nation state is part of an allied grouping such as NATO or CAS and it does not

have territorial threat perse, there would be a need to acquire desirable RMAs in areas such as offensive air power, ISR capabilities including UAVs and access to spacecraft based assets, be it communication, imagery and so on.

28. Further, as part of force multipliers and selective arming itself at considerable cost in case of rich nations and in the realm of wish list for poorer countries are RMAs based on laser technology, PGMs, UCAVs, cruise missiles and nuclear weapons, the latter subject however to an extremely sensitive non-proliferation regime in place.

Haves and Have-Nots

29. Military balance as an index of a state's capability to match its likely adversaries, deal with internal conflicts and/or to contribute its share in internationally accepted operations such as UN Peace keeping or ISAF type of missions would involve possessing RMA capability by such a state in areas as mentioned earlier in the categories of 'must', 'should' or 'could' or essential, desirable or wish list.

30. On the above basis, it is increasingly difficult for militaries in support of their national interests not to invest reasonably and incrementally in at least the essentials of RMAs e.g. BANGLADESH ARMY as the largest contributor of troops for United Nations peace keeping Operations would need to equip its soldiers with essential RMAs and at times with certain add-ons in order to stay current and credible. Israeli Armed forces on the other hand, today a world leader in cutting edge RMAs, would equip itself with not only the most sophisticated ISR aids or UCAV assets but may also like to leverage certain classified technologies in the possession of USA.

31. So, what constitutes haves? Apart from personnel and force protection, this would include surface logistics and transportation, reasonable degree of secure reliable and adequate redundancy built communications within theatre and Inter-theatre and ability to operate at night in all types of terrain and weather conditions over land, sea and air.

32. Beyond the above, only the sophisticated militaries would posses the have-not capabilities such as ability to network all operations and logistics, have a degree of air transport capability both fixed wing and rotary some of them of the armed if not attack variety of helicopters and a very high degree of inter operability with first world militaries.

33. Far beyond the above capability, USA, Russia, China and a few western nations also seek to develop and deploy PGMs capable of being fired from land, sea and air as also replace men and women with robots and networks and also use space for a 24X7 over watch for immediate response to any developing situation.

Human Resources (HR) and Man-Machine mix

34. More important than being in possession of appropriate high technology and capability per se, to be part of a RMA is the quality of men able to utilize the same to optional effect as also the trained manpower available to use and maintain such a resource. This would involve not only the military but also nation as a whole and the society, which produces or contributes to this manpower.

35. The educational and knowledge base of the supplying society, quality of its infrastructure and technical institutions, the industrial base and above all the ease of adaptation of the available manpower to apply RMA are relevant factors when we look at RMA absorption.

36. Two examples of inability at the tactical level to utilize available RMA resource to optimal use is to be mentioned. In the Indo-Pak War of 1965, Pakistan Army helped by USA was in possession of the then latest M-48 Patton tanks capable of auto fire control system, which would have proved decisive in any tank vs tank engagement against Indian Sherman and Chieftain tanks. But since Pakistani crew did not have the time to absorb the sophisticated technology and necessary skill required, these tanks became a liability and were thus made a graveyard in a village ASSAL UTTAR which was later named Patton nagar.

37. In another example of poor training, lack of technical skills and poor maintenance Iraq army though possessing Air defence capability based on contemporary Soviet equipment, showed itself in poor light in both the Gulf wars, Enduring Freedom later in 2003.

38. RMAs to be, therefore, taken advantage of must be backed by a sound knowledge and technological base of the nation state that aspires to practice the commensurate art of warfare.

Distinct effect on outcome of conflict

39. In order to comprehend the magnitude of contribution of RMAs in deciding outcomes of conflicts a few examples may be in order.

40. **American Civil War:** The defeat of the largely feudal Confederate Army at the hands of the state organized Unionists has been a watershed in RMAs, not only for superior weaponry and logistics but for military as an organized way of life, which systematically would be able to overcome opposition to it by relentless application of a greater mass of fire at points of application.

41. **Expansion and consolidation of the Ottoman Empire:** In an era dominated by the European powers at the beginning of the industrial renaissance it was a revelation for Islamist warriors with Mongolian ancestry to gradually use the very skills of warfare perfected then of mass and sudden movement of cavalry with superior logistics and backed by an armada of cannon mounted ships, to great effects. Commencing with Asia Minor which Turkey was then known as, the conscript armies of Ottomans who hired European nobility, defeated kingdoms one after another, overthrew Romans from Constantinople, renaming it as Istanbul and captured territory upto Vienna. This RMA came about as a result of greater organizational cohesion and synergy amongst various elements of an invading force. Siege warfare i.e. of starving populations and defeating elements by cunning and superior logistics was perfected then.

42. The end of the Second World War by use of two atomic bombs remains till date the biggest RMA or the mother of all RMAs and the power and sophistication of the nuclear bomb is sought to be perfected by continued miniaturization, improved delivery means, greater redundancy and precision targeting by the select group of countries who have the economic and scientific means to do so.

43. The cold war period between the USSR and its proxies and USA-led NATO provided a fertile ground to research, develop and field a number of RMAs for use mostly by surrogates such as Israel, Egypt, Syria, China, Pakistan and also India.

44. However, but for phenomenal strides in missile delivery, PGMs and ISR capabilities, apart from miniaturization of nuclear arsenal, no telling effect encompassing geopolitical changes has been effected till the end of cold war and coming in to existence

of a number of newer states in Balkans, East Timor etc. The gap between the haves and haves-not is now being felt decisively to widen giving a destructive capability and power to bring in civilizational changes to the only superpower, USA. The use of air power with PGMs and remote control of operation by use of networks with battlefield transparency has permitted targeting of single even moving targets such as a car on a highway in Riyadh by an operator of US central command in Florida.

Geopolitical Re-alignment and Emergence of Multi-Polar World

45. While Russia with its newly re-organized control over its oil and gas potential is leveraging its hegemonious clout over its near-abroad as also challenging US supremacy in world affairs, it is accepted that by middle of 21st century there are likely to be 5 or 6 power centers inclusive of India, should we play to our potential.

46. These power centers are likely to wield power and influence amongst each other by consolidating emerging technologies, and newer resources with RMAs. Control of space, Robotics, Laser based weapons, use of nano-technology and fuel cells, use of electromagnetic spectrum, miniaturization of weapons of mass destruction, all of these networked in a secure fool proof environment are likely to be the areas of intense research and domination.

47. India as part of third world group of countries, aspiring for a developed status in two decades, having a strong largely dissuasive military strategy as also matching technological prowess needs to re-focus its priorities in garnering RMAs in the future as part of its grand strategy.

48. India has therefore very little choice, other than being with the haves and put knowledge management and R&D on a firmer footing than hitherto. Opportunities for a youthful nation such as ours with a reasonable economic forecast are there for us to attain this goal. The need is for the scientific-business-industry-military community to synergise effort in this direction. The DRDO, the sword arm for R&D in Defence, has notched up certain major successes in the strategic field viz., in development of PRITHVI & AGNI series of missiles as also the ISRO has generally kept the country abreast in the area of space. Should India's specific safeguards in civilian use of nuclear energy be effected as planned, we could hope for India to be able to close this gap in RMA capability with the first world sooner than expected.

****

4

Future of Global Security: The Disproportionality Factor

*MAJ GEN VINOD SAIGHAL (RETD)**

In taped interviews to an Afghan interrogator, two Afghans and three Pakistanis, who were among 21 people, arrested earlier in 2006 described their roles in the attacks, which killed at least 70 people, most of them Afghan civilians but also international peacekeepers, a Canadian diplomat and a dozen Afghan police officers and soldiers. In the tape, the men described a fairly low-budget network that begins with the recruitment of young bombers in the sprawling Pakistani port city of Karachi. The bombers were moved to safe houses in the border towns of Quetta and Chaman, and then transferred into Afghanistan, where they were provided with cars and explosives and then sent out to find a target.

* Major General Vinod Saighal (Retd), former Director General of Military Training

Disproportionality works against the forces tackling terrorism, especially terrorism of the type taken up by radical Islamists in several countries. By now most people are fairly well acquainted with the terror breeding facilities that were set up in Pakistan and Afghanistan right up to the allied invasion of Afghanistan, following the 11/9/2001 attacks on the USA. While the Jihad factories might have collapsed in Afghanistan after the fall of Kabul in October 2001, there was hardly any let up in selected areas of Pakistan, which continues to churn out fanatical, zombie-like students in large numbers in their madarassas. The numbers of potential Jihadis can now be reckoned in the hundreds of thousands, if not in the millions, because these institutions have since spread to many other parts of the subcontinent and beyond.

The streamlined production facilities for churning out young, radicalized, possibly misanthropic students in large numbers is not a costly exercise, seeing the ready availability of young recruits from families, which although impoverished, produce children in large numbers. The average size of such families being six or seven, they are ever ready to send one, two or more children to the madarassas where they are clothed, fed and taught elementary counting besides writing in Urdu and Arabic in order to learn the *Quran* by rote. Not all of the products coming out of these madarassas would make high caliber terrorists. After very strict weeding out even if two or three were to be found fit for undertaking the type of terrorist strikes, including suicide missions that the world has come to dread, the final count would still be impressive. With variations for time, place, or the country where Jihad factories are located, the cost of training of one potential terrorist is not likely to exceed twenty thousand rupees, especially in the poorer districts of Pakistan. This works out to less than US $500 per recruit at the production site. Thereafter, translocation to other countries and proper kitting out for the task could add to the cost by several hundred or even a few thousand dollars. Except for very exceptional cases the total cost would not exceed US $5000.

Taking the case of the countries that are involved in the battle *against* global terrorism, it will be seen that compared to the training of an average Jihadi for carrying out terrorism acts, the cost of training the average soldier involved in combating this menace would be far higher. In the case of the armies of most of the countries in Asia, for example India, The Philippines or Indonesia it could be a factor of 10 or 20. That is to say that if the cost of training of an average Jihadi for undertaking terror missions works out to $5000, the cost of training of an average combatant in the countries mentioned, could work out to between 50,000 to 100,000 US dollars. In the case of USA and some of the western democracies, however, the cost increase it could be a factor between 50 and 100, especially when training of Special Forces is taken into account. These cost differentials continue even for persons rendered *hors de combat*. To elaborate: an injured Jihadi would be taken clandestinely to some sympathetic medical practitioner and operated upon in the most rudimentary fashion. In case of death the burial costs would be minimal. Terminal benefits to the family of the deceased would be a few hundred thousand rupees, equivalent to $4000 approximately. For impoverished families in Pakistan, that offer their children for such activities, even half that amount would be considered a windfall.

Match this amount of approximately $4,000 in case of injury or death for the Jihadi with the cost that would be incurred for a US soldier who becomes a casualty. For serious injuries the cost of evacuation (normally by helicopter) to an advanced field hospital and subsequently to a facility in Europe or the USA, plus the cost of treatment would work out to a differential factor between 1,000 and 10,000. For serious injuries or death the pension and terminal benefits would be an order of magnitude higher than those in the case of an injured or dying Jihadi.

The next item to be considered in this category is the cost of maintaining a Jihadi in the field as compared to a US or western soldier. Taking the Afghanistan or Iraq theatres the cost of maintaining a Jihadi in the field for one year would seldom go beyond $1000, whereas the cost of maintaining a western soldier for the same period would go up by a factor of about 100 or so depending upon the location of the soldier or his unit. Here again, Special Forces come into a separate category.

So far, the comparisons worked out related only to the training and deployment of the adversaries. We now have to consider the cost differential relating to combat scenarios.

Combat Scenarios

We move next to the cost evaluation disparities in 'live' engagements between terrorist teams and the US or NATO forces combating them. The disparity resulting from suicide missions will be taken separately at the end. Sporadic engagements between Jihadi type elements and the US forces and allies are taking place practically every day in Afghanistan and Iraq. While there may be similarities in the type of attacks carried out by the Jihadi elements in Afghanistan and Iraq the terrain conditions obtaining being very dissimilar the response patterns also vary considerably. In Afghanistan a typical incident could take any of the following forms: an IED being set off along a route where the US or International Security Assistance Force (ISAF) teams have to pass; a mortar attack at an installation or small-sized post; ambush; or hit and run operations launched from terrain that would be difficult to negotiate by foreign forces. The difficulty in terrain negotiation in mountainous country stems both from lack of the type of familiarity that local inhabitants have as also from the type of equipment used by foreign forces. In a typical ambush or hit and run operation a handful of Jihadis fire a few rockets and mortar rounds on a US convoy or position. The latter could be a temporary halting place or post occupied by a platoon-sized force. The initiative almost invariably being with the attacker (the regrouped Taliban) the opening shots in the form of various type of Small Arms (SA) would be fired from well-selected positions on the mountainside overlooking the convoy or the post. By now the retaliation procedure having also been perfected to a fine art by the US forces, the retaliation is swift. There is immediate fire in very heavy volumes on the post or the convoy attacked with integral weapons. Simultaneously the call goes out for armed helicopters and aircraft strikes. Without going into further details, tabulation can be made of the cost of the exchange to the two sides. In the case of the attackers, surprise being with the attackers, few, if any casualties would be suffered by them, after letting off their initial volleys, the Taliban escape to a more sheltered position or simply melt away. The cost of the attack on the US forces to the Taliban would not normally exceed $100. It must be noted here that there is no dearth of arms and ammunition of all types in Afghanistan. Weapons and munitions had been dumped or sent in by the Russians, Americans, Iranians and the Pakistanis in huge quantities over the years. Even now the pipeline in manpower and war-materiel from Pakistan is intact, Pakistan's frontline status in the war on terrorism is notwithstanding. The *cost of response* to even the most elementary form of attack by a handful of Taliban fighters on a US convoy or post could exceed a million dollars.

The retaliatory US exchange would normally include the following: thousands of rounds of automatic fire, dozens of rounds of rocket and mortar fire, several rounds of tank fire, hundreds of rounds of artillery fire, plus munitions and missiles unleashed from the attack helicopters, and bombs and munitions dropped by aircraft. To this not inconsiderable fire power of all types that would have been expended has to be added the fuel cost for the helicopters and aircraft called in for close support. Even without taking into consideration personnel or vehicle casualties that may have resulted in the US force - generally caught off guard, the initiative being with the enemy - the cost disparity might work out to be about one is to one million. It could become several millions should some persons become casualties or if a tank or helicopter is to be destroyed.

Coming to Iraq the situation is different. Firstly, the terrain and engagement patterns vary considerably. Much of the country is desert-like and flat, especially where the main fighting is concentrated in the Sunni triangle. While ambushes to road convoys and IED explosions can take place almost anywhere, insurgent type attacks on the US forces or their allies are mostly in built-up areas. As opposed to Afghanistan the casualties inflicted on the US soldiers, in personnel and equipment have generally been much higher. Again, varying greatly from Afghanistan, the retaliatory fire from the US forces is often of far greater intensity and longer duration. The weapons mix is also different because in Iraq the insurgents often get into buildings from where they are prepared to engage their opponents in prolonged skirmishes. The savage bombing that follows results in massive infrastructure damage. If the infrastructure damage costs were to be included the cost differential for each skirmish between the insurgents and the US forces could work out to well over 10 million to one in the US dollar terms. Excluding infrastructure damage the cost would still go up by an additional factor of three to five compared to Afghanistan.

Suicide missions belong to a separate category for several reasons. To begin with retaliatory fire is neither possible in most cases nor would it be required because the target self-destructs along with whatever other carnage that might have taken place by way of the number of people killed or wounded and the other damages resulting from the detonations caused by the suicide bomber.

The analysis given above clearly brings out that over a period of time the elements indulging in terror attacks against the US or Western forces are able to extract phenomenal costs from their adversaries, which purely in the US dollar terms result in adverse ratios varying from one is to one million or one is to several millions. Of late the number of incidents, which were already high in Iraq, have increased in Afghanistan as well. Besides manpower losses which the Western democracies can ill afford - and their opponents afford ad infinitum - the financial bleeding that takes place is something that the US and its allies can ignore only at their peril. It does not mean that technological superiority is given the go by. It indicates, however, a change in military as well as geopolitical strategy. At the operational level it requires a radical re-think in local level initiatives and the tactics adopted by the US forces and their allies in the field.

Taliban terror crippling Afghan Schools

Approximately 165 schools and colleges have been burnt down or forced to close so far by resurgent Taliban and their Islamist allies. Five years after the end of the Afghan war the Taliban seem to be back with a vengeance, one of their main targets being the country's education system. Educationists feel that the campaign is intended to terrorise families into keeping children uneducated, unemployable, and a recruitment pool for the Islamists. Teachers are the main targets. Some have been beheaded, others shot in front of their classes. One was killed while attending his father's funeral. They have declared that only madarassas meeting their approval will be allowed to operate. One of the attacks was on Kartilaya High School in the center of Lashkar Gar, the provincial capital of Helmand, which has 4,200 pupils, about half of them girls. Something similar is being attempted in Kashmir and other parts of the subcontinent. Schools are burned down, teachers beheaded and the students dealt with severely for disobeying the fiats of the radicals. Rebuilding the schools becomes a costly proposition.

Reports from the tribal areas of Pakistan, bordering Afghanistan suggest that the tribesmen fighting against the Pakistan Army could be going from strength to strength. In fact, they could be expanding their influence in adjoining districts as well. According to most analysts the situation in Pakistan's tribal badlands could be fast spiralling out of control. The Islamic radicals in Waziristan can be seen to be a part of a fast-spreading pan-Islamic movement of radical groups opposed to all those whom they consider to be enemies of Islam. The fight against the forces of *Kufr* lead by America is seen to be a long drawn out one. They are vehemently opposed to the Pakistan Army's assistance to USA in the War on Terror and might not even be satisfied with the ouster of the US forces from Afghanistan and Pakistan. The Pakistan Army who were the progenitors of the Jihadi groups are slowly losing their hold on them, after having empowered them politically in some of the states, as also in the Pakistan assembly at the cost of the mainstream political parties. Presently, the Pakistan Army continues to be the strongest force in Pakistan. Gradually, it might end up by ceding its pre-eminence and becoming the equal if not the junior partner of the Jihadis. A future reversal along these lines of the patron-client relationship between the Pakistan Army and the Jihadis could destabilize the entire region. In the short time it could also become the motive force for revitalizing and further radicalizing the Muslim *umma* worldwide.

In examining disproportionality ratios between the dispensers of global terror and the forces deployed to counter it worldwide, added security costs that have gone up considerably in several domains have to be factored. These relate to heightened surveillance at airports, railways and bus terminuses, ports and dockyards, nuclear plants, vital bridges and installations, water supplies and so many other areas of enhanced vulnerability for civilian populations. Around the world, increased security has been provided to persons considered vulnerable to targeting by terrorists or their agents. Many businesses have seen their expenses go up considerably due to increased insurance costs. The case of airlines and shipping lines has been well documented. If all the costs that have gone up due to terror strikes, especially after 9/11, are taken together the total cost worldwide could conceivably run into tens of billions of dollars, possibly exceeding fifty billion dollars annually. It has also to be noted that these are recurring costs that are likely to continue till well into the future. Putting it all together the adverse ratios that were already very high for governments and security forces dealing with terrorists go up by several orders of magnitude, if the entire spectrum of enhanced global security is taken into account. Terrorists win on two counts: massive damage to civilians and property by the acts of terror plus the disproportionality alluded to in the earlier paragraphs.

Since March 2003, the monthly cost of the war in Iraq has risen from $4.4 billion to $7.1 billion, which means that the war could cost $266 billion more than originally projected - and ultimately reach $1.2 trillion. Put in another way, Americans so far have been paying approximately $46 million per Al Qaeda operative killed. It is part of the reason for the soaring budget costs of the Defense Department. In 2002 it was $310 billion. In 2005 it swelled to $420.6 billion. The well-known Levy Institute estimates that the United States will owe foreigners $8 trillion by 2008 - a hefty 60% of its gross domestic product.

OO

Once the war-spending bill is passed, military and diplomatic costs will have reached $101.8 billion in fiscal year 2006, up from $87.3 billion in 2005, $77.3 billion in 2004 and $51 billion in 2003, the year of the invasion, according to Congressional analysts. Even if a gradual troop withdrawal were to begin in 2006, war costs in Iraq and Afghanistan are likely to rise by $371 billion during the phase-out, the report said, citing a Congressional Budget Office study. When factoring in costs of the war in Afghanistan, the $811 billion total for both wars would have far exceeded the inflation-adjusted $549 billion cost of the Vietnam War. The report details how operations, maintenance and procurement costs have surged to $88 billion this year from $50 billion in 2004, citing rising expenditures for body armour, oil and gasoline; equipment maintenance; and training and equipping Afghan and Iraqi security forces. War-related investment costs have more than tripled since 2003, to $24 billion from $7 billion, as money has been spent on armoured vehicles, radios, sensors and night-vision goggles, as well as on equipment for reorganized the U.S. Army and Marine Corps units. "These reasons are not sufficient, however, to explain the level of increases," the report says*.

❍❍

Since 2001 over 400 coalition and NATO-led troops have been killed, half of them in the past 18 months. As in Iraq, more and more have fallen victim to remote-controlled bombs and suicide attacks. It was always said of Afghans that they were not the suicidal type – until, in a dozen blasts last year, it turned out that they were. Arabs, Central Asians and, especially, Pakistanis have also blown up themselves.

Fortunately, their efforts have had limited success, but the Taliban seem to be unconcerned about their own losses. They have recently readopted the tactic of massing several scores of their fighters in ambushes, knowing that most would be killed.

"The world must find a better way to tackle the terrorism afflicting Afghanistan or the West will suffer again", president Hamid Karzai said after more US soldiers died in clashes with the Taliban. "The US-led 'war on terror' launched after the September 11, 2001 Al Qaeda attacks in the United States has largely been limited to Afghan soil but should be extended to the sources of terrorism. The international community needs to 'reassess the manner in which the war on terror is conducted'. Karzai added that he had been in discussion with Afghanistan's partners about a "change of approach".

"We can't tolerate it forever... in the past three weeks five, six hundred people have died in the country. We want an end to this, a basic end to this."**

❍❍

**The Wall Street Journal.* April 28 – May 1, 2006.

***The Times of India,* June 24, 2006

Several years earlier, CIA operatives had independently come to similar conclusions. "We've got to change the rules," the CIA's bin Laden unit chief had argued in the aftermath. It was time for the agency to try to break the policy stalemate about the Taliban. Al Qaeda was growing, and its sanctuary in Afghanistan allowed ever more ambitious operations. Within the CIA and at interagency White House sessions the Counter Terrorist Center officers spoke starkly. "Al Qaeda is training and planning in Afghanistan, and their goal is to destroy the United States," they declared, as one official recalled it. "Unless we attack their safe haven, they are going to get continually stronger and stronger.*

The logic a few years down the line can be applied in reverse. Today it is the Jihadi menace growing in the sanctuaries on the other side of the border in Pakistan that threatens the stability of Afghanistan. It will continue to grow and exact heavier and heavier toll on NATO and ISAF soldiers unless the trans-border sanctuaries are taken care of.

OO

On another occasion a UK police commissioner speaking in a Southeast Asian capital presciently said that "the threat is very grim, there's no doubt about it. There are, as we speak, people in the United Kingdom planning further atrocities".**

Yet when the conspiracy was unearthed a month later in August the potential tragedy that was prevented by rounding scores of people readying themselves for a chemical attack in several commercial aircraft, the flight disruptions and heightened security measures had already added hundreds of millions of dollars in costs to the authorities and to

---

*Daring me to Kill Them, Page no. 537-538. *Ghost Wars* by Steve Coll

**Sir Ian Blair Police Commissioner. *The Nation,* Bangkok, July 8, 2006

commercial enterprises and individuals due to the unforeseen dislocation. The multiplication of costs whenever such incidents take place, are astronomical compared to the outlays of the perpetrators of the horrors.

By not going to the source as Hamid Karzai suggested the countries fighting the Jihadi menace would always invariably remain at the receiving end. The USA along with its partners will have to set up far more effective networks to fight potential terrorists at the source rather than relying on unreliable allies of an earlier era. Intelligence operatives have long felt that the CIA and the White House had become prisoners of their alliances with Saudi Arabia and Pakistani intelligence. America was in a war against a dangerous terrorist network. As it waged that war, it was placing far too much faith in unreliable allies. The CIA needed to break out of its lazy dependence on liaisons with corrupt, Islamist-riddled intelligence services such as the ISI and the Saudi General Intelligence Department, argued one of the specialists working in the sector during the years when the Taliban were running the show in Afghanistan. If it did not, he had insisted, the CIA and the United States would pay a price.*

Others in the US saw terrorism fundamentally as "a challenge to be managed, not solved". It was felt that terrorist attacks seemed likely to become a permanent feature of American experience. The metaphor of waging "war" against terrorism was objected to because "it is a war that cannot be won" and also "unlike most wars, it has neither a fixed set of enemies nor the prospect of coming to closure." A better analogy than war might be "the effort by public health authorities to control communicable diseases." A lesson of American counter terrorism efforts since the 1980s was that the threat could not be defeated, only "reduced, attenuated, and to some degree controlled." Striving for zero terrorist attacks would be as unhealthy for

*The Kingdom's Interests, Page no. 415. *Ghost Wars* by Steve Coll.

American foreign policy as pushing for zero unemployment would be for the economy, one expert believed. In a broad sense, the expert's outlook accorded with Clinton's: Terrorism was an inevitable feature of global change.*

At another place in the book it is mentioned that Paul Wolfowitz, Bush's influential deputy defense secretary, had concluded by then that the war against Al Qaeda was something different from going after individual acts of terrorism. This was a change from how terrorism had been managed the last time the Republicans held power. Wolfowitz could see, as he recalled it, that "it really does involve all the elements of national power, that it's not just something for the intelligence community alone." As to the regional questions, he concluded it was impossible to destroy Al Qaeda "without recognizing the role that the government of Afghanistan is playing."**

Paul Wolfowitz's logic again goes to show that a few years down the line the situation in Afghanistan cannot be stabilized unless the threat from across the border is tackled. Otherwise the casualties to the coalition forces would keep mounting at disproportionately minimal cost to the opponents.

OO

That the Taliban are on a comeback trail in Afghanistan is no longer in doubt. They seem to have moved into southern Afghanistan in a big way, assassinating opponents, ambushing military patrols and generally terrorizing parts of the population opposed to them. Many US experts and defense analysts have felt that the resurgent Taliban pose a greater threat to Hamid Karzai's government at the present time than at any point since the fall of Kabul in October 2001. The insurgency in southern Afghanistan appears to be

---

**Ibid.*We are at War, page no. 433.

**Many Americans are Going to Die, page no. 565. *GHOST WARS: The Secret History of the CIA, Afghanistan and Bin Laden, from the Soviet Invasion to September 10, 2001* by Steve Coll, Penguin Books.

a loose alliance of Taliban fighters, Al Qaeda supporters and followers of Gulbuddin Hekmatyar.

Taliban commander Mullah Dadallah (now killed) reportedly told *Al Jazeera* in May 2006 that the insurgents could call on 12000 fighters. As to how and why Afghanistan seems to be again coming under the sway of the (vanquished) Taliban is a question that requires a fresh look. There is hardly any doubt that the Taliban could not have made a comeback without the tacit support of the Pakistan military establishment or, as is generally suggested by various observers, without the active help of sympathizers and rogue elements in Pakistan's ISI. For several years from 2002 to date the US has been overlooking many Pakistani transgressions. Pakistan even floated the idea of moderate Taliban for consumption by Hamid Karzai and his US backers.

There is now a belief in some circles that Osama bin Laden was allowed to escape from the Tora Bora complex after its saturation bombing. Instead of the few thousand US marines that were positioned there for mopping-up, the actual mopping up was entrusted to local Afghan warlords. Osama bin Laden, it is said, crossed into Pakistan and was whisked away by the Pakistanis, who reportedly even provided him emergency medical care. There can be little doubt that some sort of a tacit understanding was arrived at between the State Department headed by General Colin Powell and President Musharraf. It is for the same reason that the biggest nuclear proliferator of all times, A.Q. Khan was given a pardon by the Pakistani President and not handed over to the US authorities. He is still not being made available for questioning by US experts and, according to some knowledgeable sources the proliferation goes on.

The deal that might have been struck with Pervez Musharraf apparently included the disarming of some of the Afghan warlords. In the case of the militias that formed the Northern Alliance the removal of heavy weapons was completed very satisfactorily. Such was not the case for the warlords operating in southern and eastern Afghanistan. Pakistan had invested heavily in Washington lobbies to ensure that the 9/11 Commission heads – both the Republican and the Democrat heads – removed the most critical references to Pakistan's complicity from the final commission text that was released for publication. Several governments would now be interested, paying sums equivalent to those paid by Pakistan, perhaps more, to find out details of the omitted portions. This input would be of crucial importance to the Hamid Karzai government in Afghanistan.

Meanwhile, the only effective force that would have been in a position to counter the Taliban – the erstwhile militias forming the Northern Alliance, separately or conjointly - has been effectively disbanded, even demolished under American pressure. Should the US forces decide to pull out of Afghanistan or considerably reduce their presence, the Taliban would be able to occupy most areas of Afghanistan without let up or hindrance. The NATO and ISAF bases would continue to remain in isolated splendour in Kabul and a few other places. Their capacity to go after the Taliban pro-actively would become limited. The Taliban cadres, with the clandestine backing of the Pakistan establishment, would not face much difficulty in extending its sway over large swathes of Afghanistan, even in the north. Central Asian republics would again be under severe threat.

* * *

---

*Author of the books:- *Third Millennium Equipoise, Restructuring South Asian Security, Restructuring Pakistan, Dealing with Global Terrorism: The Way Forward* and *Global Security Paradoxes 2000-2020.*

5

Offsets and Indian Defence Industry

*Brig Vinod Anand (Retd)**

Offsets in the Past

Though a formal offset policy has been promulgated by the Indian government this year and included in Defence Procurement Procedure 2006 (DPP-2006) yet it cannot be said that offsets or counter trade in some forms or the other were entirely absent from the defence purchases made by India in early years. After independence India imported large quantity of defence equipments from UK, other European countries and the Soviet Union. In mid-sixties bulk of imports were from Soviet Union. In 1980s weapon systems from different sources were procured and impetus was also imparted to strengthen own defence industry

* Brig Vinod Anand (Retd) is a Senior Research Fellow at United Service Institute of India - Centre for Strategic Studies and Simulation, New Delhi.

especially Defence Public Sector Undertakings (DPSUs) along with increased R & D by Defence Research and Development Organisation (DRDO). But no formal offset arrangements or policy existed, which might have given us twin benefits of transfer of technology and enhanced investment in defence industrial sector including foreign financing and investment.

However, there were arrangements with the Soviet Union for something like barter trade, for instance purchase of defence equipment through Rupee-Ruble arrangements which saved very precious and scarce foreign exchange. Both deferred payments and savings in terms of foreign exchange reduced the adverse impact and heavy financial burden on the defence budget. Also, after importing a specific number of weapon platforms, e.g. Mig-21 jet fighters, licensed production in terms of their assembly was resorted in India. And thereafter upgrades of Mig-21 were also done through integrating French and Israeli Aircraft Industry avionics by HAL and sending the same to Russia for fitting of Russian systems and finally fitting the entire system to Mig-21 in India[1]. Thus India derived tremendous financial and increased combat value by such technology upgrades which can easily be said to be some form of offsets.

Accepting of payment in Rupees and purchasing Indian goods with these Rupees amounted to 100 percent offsets. And co-production of planes and tanks took the effective value of offsets to above 100 percent. Further, these arrangements enabled Indian defence industry to develop its own capacities which were very limited in the early years after independence. However, while the effort of importing nation is directed towards obtaining offsets, the exporting nation also strives to make the maximum profit economically and also at times strategically.

Therefore past record of India in offsets can be said to be mixed one; while long term credit and Rupee or barter trade helped India in short term, it appeared to be less effective in the long term. Though the opportunity to leverage India's defence purchases for improving its defence industrial base through offsets route existed yet the same was not fully exploited in a substantial and coordinated fashion by the Indian government.

Offsets becoming a Mandatory Norm

Because of a happy confluence of a number of factors India is now in a position to diversify its sources for defence imports. The strategic environment in favour of India has improved, its economy is on the rise and India has emerged as the largest importer of defence equipment in 2003 ($ 2953 million) accounting for 19 percent of global arms sales and beating China, another top spender in the defence field. According to SIPRI India's imports in 2003 doubled over the previous year. SIPRI's 2005 report puts India's arms imports at $ 9.5 billion over last six years, second largest after China. From the year 2000 to 2004 total arm imports by India were $ 7,526 million at 1990 constant prices[2]. And applying the current yard stick of obtaining 30 percent of direct offsets of the value of the contract in terms of transfer of technology and foreign direct investment in defence industrial sector the concomitant benefits would have been very substantial.

While the Indo-US strategic partnership was on the upward trajectory, India introduced its offset policy with the twin objectives of obtaining transfer of technology and other benefits from the international practice of offsets in the defence industry. A US Department of Commerce study of 2005 on offsets in defence trade concludes that practice of offsets in defence trade has almost become mandatory.

The US is the largest exporter of weapon systems and assorted defence equipment. Therefore, its practices in providing offsets along with the European practices of both receiving offsets as well as giving offsets besides the offsets practices of African, Latin American and other developing countries need to be studied in order to hone our skills in getting best value and worth for our newly injected offsets clause in defence import contracts.

Understanding Offsets

An offset in defence trade is an industrial compensation required by the importing country as a condition of import from the exporting country. This mandatory compensation can take several forms; it can be directly related to weapon systems being purchased and related services, or it can involve activities or goods unrelated to the weapon systems. The compensation can be further classified as a **Subcontract, Purchase, Co-production, Technology Transfer, Licensed Production, Credit Transfer, Foreign Direct Investment, or Training.** South Africa refers to offsets as Industrial Participation (IP). IP is further divided into national IP and Defence IP which again has two divisions i.e. Defence and Non-defence IP. Australia terms offsets as Strategic Industrial Defence Activities (SIDAs).

India's DPP-2006 lays down the manner in which offset obligations should be discharged and also describes in a general manner the meaning of offsets though a specific or all encompassing definition of offsets has not been given[3]. The manner of discharging offsets obligations as given below gives us an indirect definition and meaning of offsets in Indian parlance:-

(a) Direct purchase of, or executing export orders for, defence products and components manufactured by, or services provided by, Indian defence industries, i.e., DPSUs, the Ordnance Factory Board, and any private defence industry manufacturing these products or components under an industrial licence granted for such manufacture. For the purpose of defence offset, "services" will mean maintenance, overhaul, upgradation, life extension, engineering, design, testing, defence related software or quality assurance services.

(b) Direct foreign investment in Indian defence industries for industrial infrastructure for services, co-development, joint ventures and co-production of defence products.

(c) Direct foreign investment in Indian organisations engaged in research in defence R & D as certified by Defence Offset Facilitation Agency (DOFA).

An elaboration of various definitions connected with offsets would be necessary to understand the true meaning of offsets as practiced internationally. Offsets terminology has been explained in the succeeding paragraphs.

Direct Offsets: Contractual arrangements that involve defence articles and services referenced in the sales agreement for military imports. These transactions are directly related to the defence items or services rendered by the exporting defence firm and are usually in the form of co-production, subcontracting, technology transfer, training, production, licensed production, or financing activities.

Indirect Offsets: Contractual arrangements that involve defence goods and services unrelated to the defence items or services referenced in the sales agreement. The kinds of offsets that are considered "indirect" include purchases, investment, training, financing activities, marketing/exporting assistance, and technology transfer.

Co-production: Production in the importing country based upon government-to-government agreement that permits the importing nation's government to acquire the technical information to manufacture all or part of a foreign origin defence article. Co-production includes government-to-government licensed production, but excludes licensed production based upon direct commercial arrangements by foreign manufacturers.

Subcontractor Production: Production of a part or component of a foreign-origin defence article. The subcontract does not necessarily involve license of technical information and is usually a direct commercial arrangement between the foreign defence prime contractor and an indigenous producer.

Foreign Direct Investment: Investment arising from an offset agreement, often taking the form of capital dedicated to establishing an unrelated indigenous entity or expanding a subsidiary or joint venture in the importing country.

Purchases: Procurement of off-the-shelf items from the offset recipient. Often, but not always, purchases are indirect by nature. Indirect purchases are similar in definition to counter-trade, while direct purchases are analogous to buy-backs.

Technology Transfer: Transfer of technology that occurs as a result of an offset agreement and that may take the form of research and development conducted in the importing nation, technical assistance provided to the subsidiary or joint venture of Foreign Direct Investment, or other activities under direct commercial arrangement between the exporting nation's defence prime contractor and an indigenous entity.

Therefore, when the US or the European countries talk of technology transfer, collaboration, co-production, and research and development it is clearly understood, what do they mean by these terms.

Whether 30 percent offsets are good enough?

DPP-2006 contains an important provision for obtaining 'offsets' which had also been recommended by Kelkar Committee. DPP-2005 also contained a similar provision but its manner of implementation was not elaborated upon. This shortcoming has been removed to a certain extent in the DPP-2006. The provision stipulates that for all the capital purchases estimated to be above Rs. 300 crores, there will be a requirement of an 'offset' obligation. In February 2006, MOD had also clarified that only "direct offsets" would be allowed in defence acquisitions for all cases valued over Rs. 300 crores and these have to relate to co-production, joint ventures and transfer of technology for maintenance, upgrades of weapon systems purchased and investment in R&D. MOD has also allayed apprehensions that offsets would be only confined to defence PSUs or Ordnance Factories; it would be up to the defence suppliers to select their Indian partners from an approved list including private and public sector companies. One of the objectives of the offset clause is to encourage foreign direct investment (FDI) which is aimed to bring in funds and state-of-the-art technologies. Implementation of this clause in letter and spirit will go a long way in strengthening the defence sector capabilities in India.

According to the Ministry of Defence (MoD) an investment of $ 10 billion will flow into the country during the 11th Defence Plan period (2007-2012) because of the offset clause in DPP[4]. MoD has also set up a new entity, the Defence Offsets Facilitation Agency (DOFA), to facilitate and coordinate issues related to offset requirements. The multi-billion dollar Multi Role Combat Aircraft (MRCA) for 126 jet fighters would be first such deal wherein the offset clause would come into play. The requirement for offsets for MRCA has been pegged at 50 percent of the cost of the deal which has caused some consternation among the competitors. As explained earlier, the minimum requirement of offsets has been set at 30 percent. Further, the charter of DOFA also includes imparting impetus to defence exports from India[5].

There is some skepticism on the capability of our defence industry to absorb such huge offsets in the given timeframe. And then there is the question of hidden costs involved in the offsets. It has also been the experience of some countries that the offsets clause contributes to corruption. (Indian government has attempted to attenuate the aspect of corruption in defence deals by introducing a provision of signing of an **'Integrity Pact'** with the contractor). Further, indirect offsets with projects in civil arena lead to social and economic development and also contribute to other essential government goals in health, education, infrastructure and other myriad activities. Therefore there is a need to adopt a flexible approach to offset clause and a mixture of direct and indirect offsets would be appropriate to absorb such large offset credits likely to become available in the next five years and even much more during the period of 15-year integrated perspective plan of the Armed Forces (2007-2022). One estimate puts the value of offsets likely to be received during the period at $30 billion at the minimum percentage of 30 percent.

Further, there is the aspect of minimum 30 percent limit for offsets. Many countries demand much higher percentage of offsets. For example, UK demands offsets of 100 percent or more for deals over £10 million; a recent Austrian purchase of radars included offsets of 280 percent; and South Africa negotiated offsets of nearly 350 percent for an arms package in 1999[6]. Therefore, is India depriving itself of enormous benefits by asking for just 30 percent? A National Offsets Policy would be more in order to take into consideration the entire gamut of issues concerning the offsets.

In order to understand the appropriate percentage of offsets which India should demand it may be necessary to review the percentage of offsets generally demanded by other countries. These percentages have been tabulated in the chart given below. There are a number of factors which may dictate the type and form of offsets which should be demanded by the importing nations.

Analysis of International Trends in Offsets Percentages Demanded

European countries which are both offset recipients and offset givers typically demand 100 percent as offsets of the defence contracts and generally these deals are with the US and also in between themselves. Thus, if India is purchasing Scorpene submarines from France or AJT Hawks from the UK or some other armaments from Sweden, it would be quite in order to demand a similar percentage of offsets in both direct and indirect form from these countries. A 12-year study (1993 to 2004) carried out on offset activity by European nations reveals that the average offset percentages for Europe exceeded 90 percent from 1999-2003, however, it was 101 percent from 1993-2003 and during the entire period of 1993-2004 it was 99.1 percent[7]. In two cases the offset percentage was at least 200 percent. In about two dozen agreements the offset percentage specified was more than 100 percent.

Middle Eastern and Asian countries generally demand lower offset percentages as compared to the European countries whereas Canada and Latin American countries stick to the European levels of offset percentages. But recent trends indicate that non-European nations demand for offset percentages is on an upward trajectory. The above mentioned American study points out that for the period 1993-2000, the average offset requirement for non-European countries totalled only 32.5 percent; for the period of 2001-2004, however, the average offset requirement rose to 72.8 percent[8].

Besides India there are only South Korea, New Zealand and South Africa which have an official policy of demanding a minimum of 30 percent but countries like South Africa and South Korea have actually demanded much more percentages in offsets and have received the same. For instance, between the years 1999 to 2004, the average of offset requirement of South Korea from the US was 68.6 percent which was double of previous five-year period[9]. Indonesia, Malaysia and Philippines demand 100 percent offsets. It can be easily deduced that the countries with developed, technically advanced economies have demanded higher levels of offsets than the other countries. India's economy which is growing and gaining in technological strength can definitely absorb increased percentages of offsets but both in direct and indirect forms. India's infrastructure and trained and skilled workforce in both defence and civil industrial arena with a variety of defence and commercial firms would be better in distributing offset transaction to get best and synergistic value from offsets.

What should be relationship between direct and indirect offsets?

It appears that the Indian government is also contemplating a "road-map" for indirect offsets in defence purchases to take full advantage of the international practice of offsets[10]. The need for India to include sectors that go beyond defence so as to benefit from offset credits for investment in infrastructure and other sectors important to the overall economy needs no emphasis. But indirect offsets should be over and above the 30 percent of direct offsets demanded[11]. In a discussion with Shri Rao Inderjit Singh, Minister of State for Defence Production, it was clarified that 30 percent demand of Direct Offsets has been kept after reviewing the experience of other countries and India's, on capacity to absorb technology. And depending upon experience gained the percentages of offsets could even go higher[12].

Therefore, question also arises as to whether there is any relationship between percentages of direct and indirect offsets to be demanded. It would be useful to study the international offset activity to gain insights into the proportion of both types of offsets that can be demanded. From 1993-2004, direct offset transactions undertaken by the US accounted for 40 percent of the total value of offset transactions; and indirect offset transactions were almost 60 percent. The mix of direct and indirect offset transactions varies each year depending upon which countries dominated defence purchases and the related offset activities along with a number of other factors. For instance, in 2003 direct offsets provided by the US to importing nations were more than the indirect offsets and the relationship reversed in the following year.

Another way of analyzing the offset activity is to study the transactions by categories of Purchases, Subcontracts and Technology Transfer. These categories accounted for 77 percent of the total value of US offset transactions for 12 year period of 1993 to 2004. Purchases accounted for 37 percent, Subcontracts accounted for 25 percent and Technology Transfer accounted for around 15 percent of the total value. Purchases include both direct and indirect forms of offsets. Large portion of direct offsets includes the categories of Co-production, Licensed Production and Subcontracts (almost 80 percent).

Therefore, when the US business interests, their defence contractors or other supplier countries say that it may be difficult to meet the demands of Indian policy of 30 percent direct offsets then obviously they are not entirely correct. It is not in keeping with the international trends and their own dealings with European and non-European countries in the matter of offsets in the defence industry. According to the US business representatives the demand that 50 percent of the components of the MRCA (which might be purchased by India) be manufactured in India involves long, complicated and extremely difficult legal and political process where a US corporation may not get approval from the US government for Technology Transfer and production facilities in India[13].

Pros and Cons – Current Indian Policy on Offsets

According to former Defence Secretary and now Deputy National Security Advisor, Shekhar Dutt, India was looking at direct offsets as it had a good industrial base and it was in its interest that manufacturers in India should have access to high technology so that the Indian industry could join the main stream of defence industry in the world. Offsets did not mean that everything had to be made here. It would amount to a trade off, in which Indian industry undertook some work here while the associated industry abroad used Indian facilities to market the product globally. These arrangements could be sustained if the quality and the price were competitive. India had the advantage of having a large pool of technical man-power and hence the cost per man unit would be much less than the developed world and this could provide a competitive edge globally[14].

Based on DPP-2006, as mentioned earlier, a defence offset facilitation agency (DOFA) in the Department of Defence Production has already been set up. The objective is to make it as user friendly and technology based as for as possible. The DOFA would assist potential vendors in interfacing with the Indian defence industry for identifying potential offset products/projects as well as for providing requisite data and information for this purpose and hence the main function of DOFA was to facilitate implementation of the offset policy. Other functions of DOFA were: promotion of exports, providing clarifications, setting up committees and sub-groups for the studies, and engaging professional bodies for assisting its functions. The basic procedure by which procurements would take place was given in web site of the MoD.

DRDO itself is a member of DOFA and could render advice on the type of offsets preferable as the agency would have best information on the level of defence technology in India and therefore critical requirements in the technical arena. Moreover, they would assess the contents of the offset and could give their considered views on how offsets could be exploited to the maximum extent and which were the agencies, both public and private, who could develop products/technology. DRDO was aware of the complete canvas of Indian industry and knew who could absorb the technology in any particular field. They could also assist DOFA in arranging expert study groups. Moreover, they could provide the expertise with regard to technology which meant the engineering process, the design and the software including design packages and human knowledge.

As mentioned earlier the offsets were often termed *compensation, equalisers, counter-trade, and counter-balancing*. For the seller it was an unpleasant obligation. Offsets in civil aviation industry had been in vogue since HAL had bought the Boeing 747-400. HAL, as an organisation had been using offset in its own deals and had already exploited the offset to the advantage of both the seller and the buyer.

In the era of globalisation and partnerships, the offsets could be seen as an opportunity, as complementarities, used to the best advantage of the seller and the buyer and it could be a win-win situation for both. Considering the fact that Indian industry had gained world class standards in a lot of areas including aerospace, offsets needed to be seen as an opportunity and not as a liability or an obligation. There is a need to identify the core competencies, skill sets and the capacities available within the industry, so as to address the offset implementation with the right type of industry. Only then could they start projecting these capacities and capabilities to the foreign vendors who were seeking local partners[15].

India enjoyed certain advantages of manufacturing competence, technical skills and a huge reservoir of engineers, respect for intellectual property rights (IPR) backed by a strong legal system, cost leadership, widespread use of English language, quality control with an ability to conform to international standards, a financial system which was transparent and efficient, with a wide-spread banking network backed by a strong regulatory network, a stable currency and a well established stock market, and a politically strong and vibrant democracy committed to enhancing regional and global security.

On the other hand the foreign defence industry views India's offsets with certain apprehension. Indian policy had no reference as yet to **"Multipliers"**. This term means that every dollar spent could get a high credit allowed by the buying government. Multipliers were helpful in steering offset projects into higher priority technology areas or to geographical areas/locations in which the government wanted to encourage investment by the supplier for ensuring overall development. Multipliers could be applied primarily to transfer of the required technology on a ToT basis, direct investment and R&D investment. Though the view of foreign representatives during a Defence industry seminar was that 'Multipliers' could range from 1.5 to 10 yet this has not been the norm in most of the offset deals. According to the US study quoted earlier, Multipliers play a small role in the offset deals.

Penalty clause in the offset policy has also not been appreciated by the foreign prime contractors. But this is necessary because there have been many cases of non-fulfillment of offset obligation by the contractors. The apprehension of penalty need not arise because India intended to deal with the best companies in the world whose efficiency and image would preclude the use of such clause. There were many other credit arrangements and bank guarantees issues which are being examined by the government.

It has been revealed by the current Defence Minister that MoD is revising its defence procurement policy (DPP) and the new DPP would be in place by March-April 2008. The goals of new DPP would be more transparency, zero-delays in the entire arms procurement process and bringing our process in line with the best international practices. The contention of arms manufacturers that MoD's policies of allowing only direct offsets is restrictive, would also be re-examined while formulating DPP-2008[16].

What should be India's approach to offset deals?

After having discussed past and present policies and policies of the US and other countries regarding offsets some of the essential considerations for evolving National Offset Policy are:-

(a) Quality before quantity

(b) Thorough life concept (assessment based on life cycle concept)

(c) Elimination of asymmetry of information (good technological and commercial information)

(d) Skilled negotiators

(e) Focus on critical technologies

(f) Continuous audit of the implementation of offset obligations

(g) Stability and continuity in DOFA manning policies.

Conclusion

Present defence industry market is a buyer's market and the practice of offsets has become commonplace. India has introduced its formal offset policy recently in DPP-2006 and is yet to gain experience in this field. Therefore the experience of other nations is a very useful tool in evolving our own offset policy. The policy of obtaining 30 percent offsets is a viable policy to start with. But these should be direct offsets with key objective of obtaining new technologies and also enable our own strategic defence industry to develop. Obtaining 100 percent offsets has been practised by a large number of countries, thus minimum limit of 30 percent should only pertain to direct offsets and higher percentages could be asked for in the forms of indirect offsets.

Foreign prime contractors would always be reluctant to meet the offset obligations and would tend to raise costs through ingenious methods and may even violate the offset credit contracts. Therefore our policy has to be very comprehensive. Quality of offsets is more important than the quantity or percentage and we have to have commercial and technical intelligence of very high order so that we can get best vale and worth of our purchasing power. Current offset policy is not very comprehensive and gives room for flexibility which is not at all a bad thing in itself. Because both offset giver and offset receiver needs a win-win situation which is very much possible in globalized world of today. Both parties can exploit respective niches, skills and strengths of each other. India is poised on the threshold of concluding mega deals in defence arena and there is a great opportunity to give impetus to develop our defence industry. If properly implemented and enforced, offsets would propel Indian defence industry to compete with defence industries of modern nations in 15 to 20 years.

References and End Notes

1 In discussion with Gp. Capt. Anil Kumar, Senior Logistics Officer, IAF and presently Senior Fellow at United Service Institute of India.

2 SIPRI Year Book 2005

3 India's Defence Procurement Procedure-2006 is available at www.mod.nic.in

4 "Parnab to defence PSUs: Take Advantage of offset policy" *The Times of India*, New Delhi, July 8, 2006

5 For government policy see Offset Provisions at http://mod.nic.in/dpm/welcome.html

6 Swaminathan Sankalesaria Aiyar, "Offsets as Incubators". *The Economic Times*, New Delhi, May 10, 2006.

7 "Offsets in Defense Trade–Tenth Study", U.S. Department of Commerce, Bureau of Industry and Security, December 2005.

8 Ibid

9 Ibid.

10 Speech by Defence Minister Mr.Pranab Mukherjee at the inauguration of 3rd Indo-US Economic Summit, New Delhi September 13, 2006. Also see "Signs of Pause in reforms, says Mulford", *The Hindu*, September 14, 2006.

11 For an American view see the US–India Business Council report of November 2005 available at http://www.usibc.com/documents/NovemberEditionFinal%20(small).pdf

12 Author's discussion with Shri Rao Inderjit Singh, Minister of State for Defence Production on October 12, 2006 during National Seminar on "Public-Private Partnership in Defence: Problems and Prospects" at Observer Research Foundation, New Delhi.

13 See N.11

14 Shekhar Dutt, Defence Secretary, during his address at Workshop on "Implementation of Offsets in Defence"

held on July 27, 2006 under the aegis of Confederation of Indian Industry.

15 In discussion with Lt. Gen. VK Kapoor (retd.) who has authored, "India Implements Offsets in Defence–A Report", published in SP Guide Publications, monthly magazine September 2006.

16 "Arms Procurement Policy to be More Transparent", *The Times of India*, October 20, 2007.

* * *

6

Defence Procurement in India – as I see it

*Dr. Yogendra Narain, IAS (Retd)**

Defence procurement in India conjures up images of shady defence agents trying to sell their hardware, through corrupt officials and sometimes corrupt politicians. The reports of the Comptroller and Auditor General on such transactions, highlighting some defects in the procedures followed in purchase of high value defence goods, immediately raises suspicions. The media adds grist to the mill and one has a perfect *pot pouri* of a scandal emerging out of every such defence transactions. Hours and hours devoted on negotiations by the officials go wasted, leaving a shattered bureaucracy, as they prepare exhaustive answers to the accusations that follow.

The reports of the Comptroller and Auditor General highlight defects of every department year after year, but it

* Dr. Yogendra Narain, IAS (Retd) was Defence Secretary, Govt. of India

is the reports on the Ministry of Defence that attract maximum attention and comments.

Based on the reports of the CAG as well as the CVC, the Ministry of Defence keeps on improving its procedures, changing the procurement manuals, tightening the financial scrutiny but yet, year after year the CAG reports highlight new deficiencies. Every Government that comes into power, highlights the improvements it has made and shows the previous Government in a poor light. Nevertheless the CAG reports continue to highlight new scandals and the blame game goes on.

Can we ever say that we have the perfect procedures in place? No.

The first major attempt to amend the procurement procedures was after the Bofors contract. Defence agents were banned and prohibited from participating in the negotiations. It was a knee jerk reaction to say the least. But this step became necessary because of the political furore that had followed it.

Some years later the CVC came in with the diktat that negotiations should only be carried out with the lowest tenderer i.e. L1. In the years that followed only minor changes in the procedures were made. Then came the CAG report on the defence procurements made during the Kargil war and immediately thereafter. The Group of Ministers, which went into the lapses during the Kargil war recommended changes in procurement procedures. They felt that these procurements should be done by a specialised body which would have the advantage of an institutional memory. Accordingly, the year 2001-2002 saw the establishment of the Defence Acquisition Council headed by the Defence Minister, the Defence Procurement Board headed by the Defence Secretary, the Defence Production Board headed by the Secretary Defence Production, and the Defence Research Board headed by the Secretary, Department of Defence Research. Each of these boards had the Vice Chiefs of the Army, Navy and the Air Force as members. Their inclusion was an essential part of the post Kargil reforms, as the Defence forces had always felt, left out in the process of procurement and negotiations.

Post Pokharan, the need was felt to expeditiously procure some essental equipment. Since there was no accepted mechanism for the same, a fast track procedure was evolved for the purpose in consultation with the Ministry of Finance, and approval of the cabinet was taken. This issue had also cropped up during the Kargil war, when in the midst of the war, the Defence Ministry suddenly found that the procedures prescribed for normal times could not be followed, when the procurement of arms and supplies has to be done on an emergent basis. We cannot afford to lose a war because of long winding procedures—an excuse which no nation would ever accept.

The setting up of the Defence Procurement Board succeeded in speeding up the process of procurement. In the first year itself, even though some money was surrendered by the Ministry of Defence, the expenditure on capital account went up by thirty percent. This was quite an achievement considering the demoralisation that had set in after the Tehelka exposures.

In the days when India was making heavy purchases from the Soviet Union, prices of weapon systems was often decided on the 'political basis'. Russia saw India as part of its camp in the Cold War even though India loudly proclaimed its non-alignment policy and was willing to supply defence equipment at what then became known as 'Friendship prices'. Russia was wooing India and India did not have many countries to choose from, as the other major supplier, i.e. USA was not too keen to participate as a supplier of defence equipment to India.

This changed in 2001, when the USA decided to develop closer defence relations with India. As part of this closeness India asked the USA to supply certain equipments which we had decided to procure from the USA before the Pokharan tests. These were the Weapon locating Radars. Pakistan already had them and was using them successfully in Siachen and other sectors. Pakistan was happily securing arms from both China and the USA and was thus ahead of us in certain areas though not in totality. The Special Secretary (Acqusitions) of India was sent to the USA to finalize the deal supported by able negotiators. Still stung by the Tehelka exposures it was decided to adopt a government to government procurement procedure, where the US government did the bidding and processing of the bid and then associated Indian team in the final negotiations.

On the other hand the Russians were adopting a tough stance on procurement of spares. Since we were heavily dependent on them for supplies of spares for the equipment we had purchased from them [Russians have supplied about 70% of the equipment for the Armed forces of India], they began to assert monopoly pressures. In 2002 when OP Parakaram started, the Air Force found that a substantial part of its fleet would remain grounded till we could get the spare parts needed from Russia. Before the break up of Soviet Russia, these parts were being supplied by the constituent states of the USSR. Though they [the individual states] were willing to supply these parts, Russia warned India that if it did buy from these independent states then Russia would not guarantee the genuineness of these parts and if some accident occured they would not be responsible. They advised India, rather aggressively, to buy the spare parts from Russia only.

The price of these spare parts in certain cases were hiked by almost 100 percent. However, since they were urgently required, a special team headed by a Joint Secretary and fully empowered, was sent from India in January 2002 to negotiate and purchase the spare parts at the best prices that could be agreed to. There was no other alternative.

The structural reorganisation , as recommended by the GoM, ensured that the concerned arm of the Armed forces was fully involved in the purchases. The negotiating committee that was set up for each procurement, consisted of the Joint Secretary of the MoD dealing with the purchase, the Deputy Financial Adviser fom the Department of Defence Accounts and a Major General rank officer or equivalent from the concerned wing of the defence forces. This has worked very well from all counts.

The increased financial delegation made to the Defence Ministry, for purchase of capital equipment alse helped in expediting the purchases. The capital expenditure and utilisation of funds suddenly shot up and in the subsequent years reached almost the entire allocations made in the budget for such capital purchases.

The Defence Ministry, wanting to get rid of the criticism of the CAG and the CVC in 2001-2002, suggested to both these organisations that to ensure more transparency and acceptability, in defence purchase, it would be helpful if all purchases above 75 crores could be first vetted by both of them, before the actual order was placed on the concerned firm. However this proposal was rejected by both of them.

Setting up of the Defence Procurement Board, has immensely helped in setting up an institutional memory on such purchases. Negotiators of the Defence Ministry now have the advantage of knowing the prices at which similar purchases were made in the past. They would also be able to know the history and past performance of the party they want to contract with.

All said and done, the defence procurement procedures now in place, are quite elaborate and adequate. There is no way price negotiations can be influenced either by politicians or other external agencies. Furthermore, the intensive scrutiny by the Defence Accounts, both during negotiations as well as post negotiations, ensures fairness and justness. If defence agents still give money to politicians or intermediaries then it is somewhere beyond the system.

If, however, further openness is required in defence procurement then perhaps it would be appropriate to follow the Australian system. In that country, every defence procurement done above a certain value, is duly notified in the gazette and is open to all citizens. The price and the company from which it has been purchased is also stated. It is a moot point however, whether all defence purchases made by India should be made open. We have a threatened security environment. Though it is true that Janes Year Book and other compilations meticulously monitor all such transactions, made by various countries but whether India should do so voluntarily is an issue to be decided; by the ruling party in consultation with the opposition. So far information relating to defence procurement can be denied under the Right to Information Act under Section 8 which provides the exception on grounds of national security.

It is significant to note though the hue and cry after the Bofors gun purchases, the presence of defence agents was banned but the CVC Sri Vittal in 2001 strongly recommended the reintroduction of agents in a regulated manner. He was practical enough to realise that all defence transactions cannot be carried out with the companies directly. The major defence companies are bidding in contracts all over the world and it is not possible for their CEO's or their officers to come directly for the negotiations.

The Defence Ministry, acting on the advice of the CVC did frame rules and regulations for the registration of agents in 2001. But there was very poor response. The feedback was that no agent wanted to give information on the commission he would get. Today the position is only slightly better.

What is the way ahead?

Many experts have suggested that defence procurement should not be done by the Defence Ministry but by a separate organisation outside the Ministry, to avoid criticism and direct involvement of the Government. They feel that this procurement could be done by an organisation working at the level of the Armed Forces Headquarters. However, this would be an escapist strategy and considering the present atmosphere surrounding defence procurement it would be doubtful if the defence forces would like to take this job on their own shoulders.

It would be appropriate, however, to set up an independent experts committee consisting *inter alia* of retired officers of the CAG and the CVC as well as retired officers of Defence and the Ministry to vet all such transactions above a certain amount, let us say 75 crores. This committee should be headed by a retired judge of the High Court/ Supreme Court and only after it clears the transaction from the procedural point of view, the contract should be signed. This would give confidence to the officers negotiating the transaction and also ensure, that if the procedures have not been followed inadvertantly, that could be corrected before the contract is approved.

To ensure accountability and to develop expertise in the Public Accounts Committee of Parliament while making a financial scrutiny of the lapses, pointed out by the CAG in defence purchases, it would be appropriate if—

[1] the report of the CAG is not made public till the PAC, after hearing both the CAG and the officers, has given its findings. Only the final report of the PAC should be made public.

[2] A separate sub-committee of the PAC should be constituted to examine the CAG reports on defence which could then build up expertise in handling such issues and could come up with well considered views to improve systems and procedures.

These steps, if taken, would prevent trial by media even before the report is considered by the PAC and prevent demoralisation of the officers.

Often delay in procurement also takes place because the Chief changes and then the entire view of the concerned arm of the defence forces changed. Without elaborating further it would only be relevant to state that it happened in the case of the purchase of the Advance Jet Trainer also. It would help if the Armed forces do not change their views with the change of guard at the top.

Our defence procurement has been adversely affected when political parties begin using the CAG reports to hit their political opponents. The officers involved unnecessarily get into controversies and their morale dips. While our neighbours have speedily improved their armoury, we are still plodding slowly but not steadily. India is a vast and big country with a vital role to play in this part of the world and it cannot afford to be a straggler any more.

Should defence procurement be linked to foreign policy? This is a policy followed by some major powers like the USA and China as well as Russia. However, it would not be wise for India to do so since we are making our policy more broadbased than ever before.

* * *

7

Network Centric Warfare— A Decisive Warfighting Advantage

*Lt Gen SRR Aiyengar, PVSM, AVSM, VSM (Retd)**

"Network Centric Warfare (NCW) provides a new conceptual framework with which to examine military missions, operations and organizations. It is intended to provide a fresh perspective to help ensure that new approaches and solutions will not be constrained by outmoded ideas."

(From CCRP publication titled 'NETWORK CENTRIC WARFARE' by David S. Alberts, John J. Garstka and Frederik P. Stein.)

---

* Lt Gen SRR Aiyengar, PVSM, AVSM, VSM (Retd)
Former Commandant of National Defence College, New Delhi, Defence Services Staff College, Wellington (Nilgiris) and Military College of Telecommunication Engineering, Mhow (MP).

Introduction

1. Network Centric Warfare (NCW) has been cited as "the emerging theory of war" and is poised as one of the key enablers of future combat power. The theory of network centricity and the numerous alternative versions it has spawned has been central to military thinking and the development of military doctrine especially after the Gulf War of 1991. Some of the world's technologically advanced armed forces are adopting NCW in its various manifestations. It is a reasonable proposition, that better the information you have about your own situation and that of your opponent, particularly if it is superior to his information, the more likely you can get inside the OODA (observe, orient, decide, act) loop and be in a better position to dictate the course of events. By achieving this information superiority, you will be able to act faster and better. Or, in other words, you will be able to seize the initiative.

2. The key to this is the availability of information—the right information, at the right time, in the right place, in the right format. This can be achieved; the argument goes, by establishing a comprehensive network around which the information can flow without hindrance, seamlessly allowing access by whoever needs it to whatever data is available. Yes, it is particularly good on Power Point slides with sensors and users linked by 'lightening bolts', and possibly in somewhat fictional descriptions of future scenarios describing smooth, error-free episodes of collaborative planning, based on exhaustive information leading to successful execution. Few leading military analysts are questioning the assumption that networking automatically leads to information superiority. As it is said that this will be true only if the enemy lays himself to be observed. A war is shaped by human nature, the complexities of human behaviour and its limitations and physical limitations. Equally true is the fact that the outcome of any war cannot be predicted with certainty because so many intangible elements are integral part of it. To believe, that war can be conducted,

as a well designed and developed machine would be gross undermining of the critical role leadership plays at all levels of war.

Fundamentals of NCW

3. NCW has been referred to a new form of warfare, an increased combat power focussing on the networking the classic domains of warfare namely, **'Physical'**, **'Cognitive**, and **'Information'**. In a fully developed conceptual model, the relations of these domains would appear somewhat as described below:-

- **Physical Domain**. Physical domain is the traditional domain of warfare. It is the domain where strike, protect and manoeuvre takes place across the environments of ground, sea, air and now space. Comparatively the elements of this domain are the easiest to measure, and consequently, combat power has traditionally been measured primarily in this domain. Two important metrics for measuring combat power in this domain, lethality and survivability, have been and continue to be cornerstones of military operations research.

- **Cognitive Domain**. Cognitive domain as the very name suggests is the domain of the mind of the war-fighter and the supporting populous. This is the domain where battles and wars are won and lost. This indeed is the domain of intangibles: leadership, morale, unit cohesion, training standards and experience, situational awareness, and public opinion. This is the domain where tactics, techniques and procedures reside. Much has been commented and written about this domain and the key attributes of this domain have remained constant over the years. The attributes of this domain are difficult to measure and each sub-domain i.e. each individual mind is unique. Consequently, explicit treatment of this domain in analytical models of warfare is few.

However, a methodology that begins to address key attributes and their inter-relationships has been and is being researched.

- **Information Domain**. Information domain is the domain where information resides. It is where information is created, manipulated and shared. It is the domain that facilitates the communication of information between war-fighters. It is also the domain where the command and control of modern military force is exercised, where commander's intent resides. Consequently, it is increasingly the domain that is to be protected and defended to enable a force to generate combat power. And, in all – important battle for information–superiority, the information domain is the 'Ground Zero'. The networking of the force changes the topology of the war-fighters information domain. It extends the existing domain and provides access to a new region, to a new operational envelope. The new operational envelope corresponds to the "network–centric" region of the information domain. Within this region resides the information constructs that are enabled by the network constructs such as the 'common operational

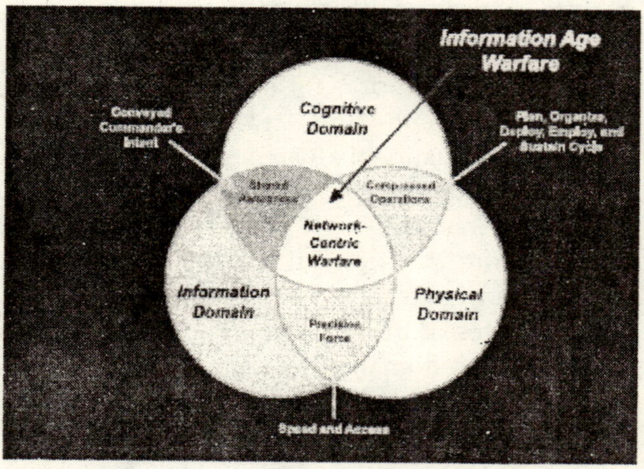

picture'. Operating within the network centric region of this domain allows war-fighters to achieve an information position that was not previously feasible or possible. Intuitively, war-fighters understand that a relationship exists between information and combat power. However capturing and quantifying this relationship has been, and continues to be, an analytical challenge.

4. A graphic representation of these domains is shown on last page. The domain intersections represent dynamic and vital areas of Information Warfare (IW). NCW exists at the centre where the three domains intersect.

Tenets of NCW

5. NCW is military operations that are enabled by the fully integrated applications and information networking of the force. It dramatically increases the combat effectiveness and efficiency through self-synchronization across the host of entities operating on the network. The tenets of NCW are:-

(a) A robustly networked force improves information sharing.

(b) Information sharing and collaboration enhances the quality of information and shared situational awareness.

(c) Shared situational awareness enables self-synchronization and collaboration and enhances sustainability and speed of command.

(d) These, in turn, dramatically increase mission effectiveness.

6. As an 'emerging theory of war', NCW is a new approach to how we might fight and conduct future warfare by 'effectively linking knowledgeable entities in battle space'. NCW is the organizing principle that guides the military's adoption of information technologies and its adaptation to these technologies. The full implications and consequences

of achieving a robustly networked force and of adopting network centric concepts of operation will, of course, need some more experimentation in developing and refining concepts and doctrine for such operations.

7. NCW concepts stress the quality of information, collaboration, and awareness and shared situational understanding to enable integrated battlefield activity in terms of survivability, lethality, speed, timeliness and responsiveness. Network centric operations are closely linked to the emerging new technologies and their close interlocking associated with Sensors, Information Technology (IT) and Weapons development. A brief resume of these three emerging technologies would be useful in understanding the ushering of NCW.

8. **Sensor Technology**. Two revolutionary developments are underway namely the move toward sensors that facilitate achieving a comprehensive, near-real time surveillance over extended areas and along with it the development toward smaller, cheaper and variety of sensors that can be netted to detect, locate, identify and track targets of concern. Acoustic, Seismic, Infrared, Thermal to name some of the type of sensors lend themselves to be integrated and fused to provide high quality of data, thus creating 'situational awareness' very precise in nature as well as 'global' in scope. These sensors are deployed in NCW scenario to form what is being referred to as the "Sensor Grid". This Grid would envelop all the mediums namely Ground (land), Sea, Air and Space.

9. **IT.** IT has been described as the DNA of the Information Age – the fundamental building block of dominant competitors. A 'system of systems' approach enabled by the advances in IT provides the network backbone and facilitates the 'Sensor Grid' to optimize on not only expanding the potential of each of the sensor deployed but allows interacting and building on one another's efforts and potential. The scope and scale of such integrated data would also dictate the need for a higher and faster computing

power to process, collate and analyze the resulting quantity of sensor data. This collated data need to be also distributed to any 'shooter' anywhere in the battle space at near-real time speeds. IT revolution must facilitate the means of ensuring both that the 'right information' reaches the 'right decision maker' at the 'right time', and the decision maker can make the best use possible of it in executing command intent. The transition from 'platform centric' cpmputing to 'network-centric' computing has been largely enabled by the recent key developments in IT.

10. **Weapons Technology**. Violence and conflict have been a feature of human life throughout history. Starting with simple weapons, people have developed ever more advanced methods to kill one another. Technology has dominated warfare since the early 1900s, and an astounding 190 million people may have been killed during the 25 biggest conflicts of the 20th century. Today guided weapons, like "smart" bombs dropped by stealth bombers, coupled with space-based sensors and precision satellite navigation, provide decisive advantages in conventional warfare. In this high-spending game, less capable opponents are soon reduced to guerrilla tactics, and human cost of war remains high. The US has embraced 'Full Spectrum Dominance', the belief that superior technology in all fields guarantees victory, though critics disagree. This has led to ever more sophisticated and expensive aircraft and a proliferation of unmanned systems, including robot aircraft to attack targets. Future plans may include swarms of flying robots, while an existing desert race for driverless vehicles may pave the way for autonomous supply vehicles. In the post 9/11 action taken against Taliban Militia and Al Qaeda supporters, the number of 'Precision Guided Munitions (PGMs)' used rose to 60% of ordnance dropped. As technology advances, so does the overall capability of weapon systems. We now have the new "Thermo-baric" bomb tested in the caves of Afghanistan, which can destroy weapons stockpile without the deadly agents being released into the atmosphere. Similarly, as the single shot kill probability of PGMs grows

steadily, the costs are reducing and future wars are likely to witness an even greater use of PGMs and specialist warheads on the battle-field.

11. The real impact of these technologies upon warfare is derived from the synergies of combining different technologies drawn from different revolutions. The improvement in the US military's capability to compress the engagement cycle (the time between target identification and attack) and to strike deeply buried targets such as command bunkers, even as the adversaries seek to use target–camouflage and mobility had been made possible due to net-centricity. In short, NCW can best be described as the combination of emerging technologies, tactics, techniques and associated procedures to create decisive war fighting advantage enabling the following distinctive features:-

- An information superiority enabled concept of operations that describes the modern technologically advanced Armed Forces would organize and fight in the Information age.
- Generation of increased combat power by networking sensors, decision makers and shooters to achieve shared awareness, increased speed of command, high tempo of operations, greater lethality, increased survivability, and a high degree of self - synchronization.
- Translation of information superiority into combat power by effectively linking friendly forces within the battle space, providing a much improved shared awareness of the situation, and enabling more rapid, effective decision making.

Network Centric Operational Architecture

12. The NCW architecture can be thought of as an integration of three functionally separate, but interoperable "Grids". These Grids are ***the Information Grid, the Sensor Grid*** and ***the Shooter Grid.***

13. **The Information Grid.** The Information Grid provides the physical infrastructure for network centric computing and communications. It provides the means to receive, process, transport, store, and protect information for the combat forces. The Grid permits the plug and play of sensors and shooters. The Grid exists in space, in the air, on land and at sea. It is a 'network of networks' comprising of communication highways, computational nodes, operating systems and information management systems that facilitate network centric computing and communication across the battle space. The Grid consists of both dedicated military and commercial communication capabilities, thereby permitting transmission of multiple information types in multiple modes at varying data rates. Another striking feature of this Grid is in its in-built information protection. The combination of all these features and capabilities results in an assured high-speed access to the information required to dominate across the entire spectrum of conflict be it of low, medium or high intensity.

14. **The Sensor Grid.** It is the collection of sensors that contribute to battle space awareness by feeding data into the Information Grid. It is composed of air, sea, ground, space and cyberspace based sensors integrated as a grid linking both platform based sensors as also sensors operated by individual soldiers and any other embedded sensors. Such an integrated grid provides all the information available to friendly forces, opposing forces and the environment across the battle space. It provides the force commander at all levels with operational capabilities essential for achieving battle-field awareness across the entire battle space. The improvement in operational capability is sought to be achieved by/through a combination of dynamic sensor tasking, reliable data fusion and effective dissemination of information over the Information Grid. By its very nature of functioning, the Sensor Grid application would include all associated software applications of sensor peripherals, their multi-mode tasking and more importantly data fusion protocols.

15. **The Engagement / Shooter Grid.** This Grid enables the planning and execution of combat operations based on information gained from the Information Grid. The Shooter Grid is like the Sensor Grid in that its constituent parts are physical, but the Grid is virtual. The shooters are tasked to create the necessary effect on the battle-field and dynamically retasked as warranted. The operational capabilities thus achieved enables the emerging concepts of precision engagement, dominant manoeuvre and full dimensional protection.

16. A logical model for Network Centric Warfare would appear as shown below. It can be discerned from this model, the 'Information Grid' enable the operational architectures of the 'Sensor and Shooter' Grids. Sensor Grid rapidly generates high levels of battle space awareness and synchronizes awareness with military operations. Shooter Grid exploit this awareness and translate it into increased combat power. However, to ensure interoperability, all the elements of the grid must be compliant with an agreed and well coordinated information infrastructure common operating environment.

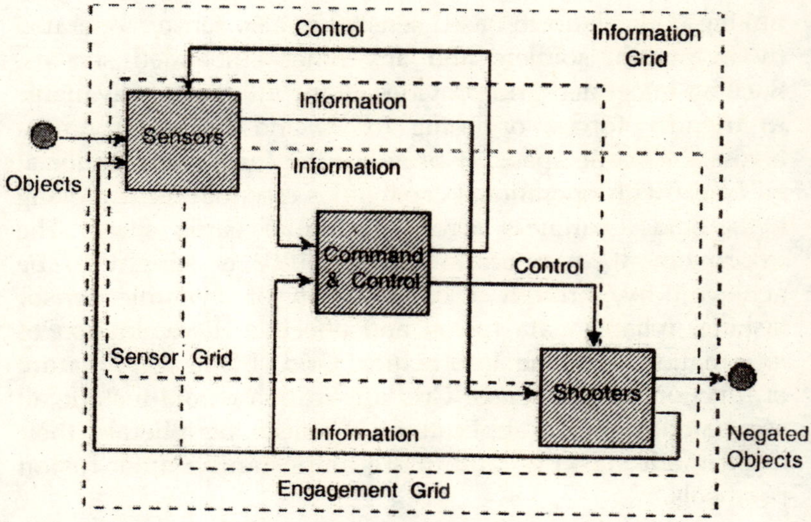

Fig. Logical Model of NCW

NCW in action: Few Examples

17. Forces that are networked, outfight forces that are not, everything else being equal. Evidence of the power of NCW, collected from a wide range of US military activities which include combat operations, training events, tests, exercises, and demonstrations strengthens and reinforces the tenets of NCW as described in the preceding paragraphs. Few examples highlighting the impact or the benefit accruing from NCW is briefly enumerated below.

18. In early October 2001, not quite a month after the 9/11 attacks on the World Trade Center, the Pentagon and in Pennsylvania, the US and British ships and aircraft introduced the 21st century (and the Taliban) network-centric operations. With a striking blend of old and new technology, operating throughout the electromagnetic spectrum and across the range of operations, from ground forces to air and sea platforms and into space, the US forces in both conflicts used networked information to achieve huge efficiencies in combat. The "kill chain" against enemy targets was reduced in many cases from hours to minutes, and information about the location of enemy and friendly forces was relayed and tracked quickly. In Afghanistan, the deployment of American ground troops was minimal; in Iraq, a force one-quarter the size of the 1991 Desert Storm coalition defeated the Iraqi regime in 21 days, with only 161 troops killed in action. In both theatres, the incidence of civilian casualties and other collateral damage was minimal.

19. **Small ground units, strategic bombers, and precision weapons = close air support**. One lingering image from Afghanistan illustrates NCW's potential, even when using old technology: a Special Force soldiers on horseback sends targeting data from his laptop computer to a 40-year-old B-52H Stratofortress, which delivers a devastating blow to massed Taliban forces in less than 20 minutes. In operations against the Taliban and Iraqi forces, B-52s and other aircraft were armed with the Joint Direct Attack Munitions (JDAM), a 2000-pound bomb with a receiver that uses in-flight

updates from Global Positioning System satellites to strike within a few feet of their aim points. Special Operations Forces on the ground used binoculars equipped with laser range finders to determine a target's exact location, and then transmitted precise coordinates to the bombers above them. Bomber crews could then program JDAMs and deliver them to targets within minutes of identification.

20. This ability to network real-time cueing from manoeuvring ground forces and a range of the sensors to the aircraft and, in turn, to the bombs themselves, put massive, accurate, and close-in fire support at the disposal of the US and Coalition troops. Often the enemy was hit with lethal and accurate firepower, not from an armoured division and thousands of the US troops, or massed formations of aircraft, but by handful of soldiers transmitting electrons to a single aircraft. Strikes that took hours to coordinate in Desert Storm, a decade earlier were carried out in Afghanistan and Iraq as quickly as 45 minutes from the time a target was identified. Many carrier-based strike missions were not even targeted until the aircraft were underway.

21. **Long-range Unmanned Aerial Vehicles (UAVs), controlled from afar = Strategic Intelligence, Surveillance and Reconnaissance (ISR).** Flying at altitudes of upto 60,000 feet, at high speed, the Air Force's experimental, high-flying, long-range Global Hawk UAV provided constant coverage of wide areas of territory and added significantly to the imagery provided by satellites and other surveillance aircraft. With its synthetic aperture radar, electro-optical camera, and infrared (IR) and other sensors, Global Hawk saw through most environmental and battlefield conditions, and provided thousands of images for use in bomb damage assessment, fire support, and general reconnaissance. From a networking standpoint, Global Hawk showed two especially unique capabilities: it was controlled through a communications network based from ground stations thousands of miles away, in Europe and California; and it

flew not only pre-planned flight paths, but also in real time to locations as required by various missions.

22. **Responsive UAVs, in support of manoeuvr forces.** The lower-altitude Predator UAV played a network-centric role by linking with RC-135 Rivet Joint, U-2, and E-8C Joint STARS ground surveillance aircraft to enhance the battlefield picture for commanders. The Predator's radar and IR sensors allowed it to see through bad weather and at night. Its video capability allowed it to transmit live images to command centers, other aircraft, or tactical controllers on the ground. These features made it invaluable to reconnaissance and manoeuvr forces engaged in combat with a moving enemy, or aircraft seeking to locate mobile targets. They also allowed the Predator, like Global Hawk, to add considerably to the overall battlefield picture available to commanders. Predator's unique network-centric contribution was in serving as "eyes and ears" for manoeuvring ground forces. For example, in March 2002, Special Operations teams in Operation Anaconda in Afghanistan were linked directly to Predators, which they used to essentially "walk point," identifying possible enemy locations or conversely, indicating when the way ahead was clear. By networking with Predator, forces could move faster than if they had been forced to deploy their own scouts to detect threats in their path, and could better employ supporting fires during their advance.

23. **A Word of Caution.** It is risky to draw too many conclusions from the Coalition's success against Taliban and Iraqi troops, simply because both adversaries were inferior in every way. One does not slight the American war fighter to observe that this was not a close fight between evenly matched forces. In military parlance, enemy forces created very little "friction" and "fog" for the US Central Command (CENTCOM) to contend with during major combat operations. Yet as the ongoing conflict in both theatres makes clear, NCW may improve what technology already does, but it cannot do things technology cannot — such as

occupy ground, protect patrolling troops from exploding mines and improvised explosive devices, or give skittish locals the feeling of security they need to come out and vote. Key aspects of leadership and the "art of war," such as intelligence, training, and command initiative, can be assisted by a network, but they cannot be replaced by one. Likewise, while network-centric operations are sustained by information and data, they have not reduced combat leadership to a process of quantitative calculations. In short, as a technology-based process, networking can neither replace, nor succeed without, many other less tangible, human aspects of waging war. Also on the flip-side of the coin, recent military operations have highlighted substantial shortcomings. First, unless properly managed the amount of information may overwhelm the commander and staff. Second, the most important information may be difficult to distinguish from trivial data. Third, as higher commanders have access to better and faster information and knowledge, they may be tempted to micromanage subordinates actions. Fourth, the concept concentrates on the science of control while neglecting the art of command. And, fifth, NCW frequently ignores the role of the commander. Regardless of the 'gizmos' available, command of soldiers remain an affair of the heart, and personal presence achieved by persistent battle–field circulation is an absolute necessity.

NCW Myths

24. Perceptions of countries about network centric warfare and capabilities thereof differ depending upon the role that they expect their armed forces to play. The application of information technology in achieving military aims and in conducting military operations also differs from country to country. Physical network infrastructure and networking concepts of each country are different. Therefore, each country has coined its own term to denote network centric capabilities. These terms thus indicate the conceptual difference that exists in this field. Network_centric, thus, is an umbrella term. Following are the terms used by various countries in this aspect:-

- US: Network Centric Warfare (NCW).
- UK: Network Enabled Capability (NEC).
- Australia: Network Centric Warfare (NCW)/Network Enabled Capability/Knowledge Analysis Framework.
- Japan : Network Centric Warfare.
- China : Informationalisation.
- NATO: NATO Network Enabled Capability (NNEC).
- Sweden: Network Based Defence.

25. Certainly there is no shortage of exaggerated claims, unfounded criticisms, and just plain misinformation about this subject. Sorting out fact from fancy will be among the community's principal tasks as we grapple with how to apply network-centric concepts to military operations. A number of myths are currently circulating about the nature, limitations, and dangers of NCW. These so-called 'myths' would need to be addressed before one gets down to detailed exploration of its applicability under all conditions. The skeptics of NCW also view the virtues of NCW in a different light cautioning a blind assimilation of the concept.

26. **Myth1: NCW is all about the Network.** IT is and has undergone a fundamental shift from platform centric computing to network centric computing. This shift is what the proponents of NCW claim that makes it a more dynamic and most effective way of conducting war. Hence, most probably the dazzle of high quality networks gives the impression that the lynchpin of NCW is the networks. Swift and effective use of information is central to the success of NCW. NCW will rely on rich situational awareness provided by persistent intelligence, surveillance and reconnaissance to sense hostile capabilities and trigger rapid and precise attacks. The vital asymmetric advantage of information superiority will, it is claimed, increase responsiveness and survivability to disperse while focussing offensive and defensive firepower over tremendous distances. Seen from the above distinct advantages to a networked force, it will

be apparent that the NCW is more about networking than networks. NCW is certainly not turning the battle over the 'network' or even about relying more on automated tools and decision aids. Networks are only the medium facilitating the effective linking of knowledgeable entities that are geographically or hierarchically dispersed. It is the ability to move information around the network and use it effectively that represents the 'revolution'. It is not the network itself that provides a solution but what it enables the user to do, at whatever level. The network must serve the needs of those engaged in operations across the spectrum of warfare, sometimes simultaneously.

27. **Myth 2: NCW will change the nature of warfare.** The study of war reveals that its conduct is influenced by certain broad precepts, which have come to be recognized as the 'Principles of War'. These principles have proved to be enduring, despite changes in technology, which have affected the application of these principles without detracting their general validity. NCW has not altered in a major manner, any of these conceptual components of military doctrine informing the conduct of operations though it has and it does question its applicability and relative importance. The evolving nature of the battle-field and the growing political constraints on warfare bring several principles under question. The increased reliance on precision munitions raises doubts about the common application of 'Mass'. And more recently the Coalition Forces campaign in Iraq, which included diplomatic, economic as well as military efforts, raises new issues with respect to 'unity of command' versus 'unity of effort'. 'Simultaneity' properly exploited seems to be gathering some importance to be added as an additional principle of war. While combined arms and attacking from different directions concurrently are as ageless as human conflict, achieving simultaneous effects easily feasible with NCW, has assumed a more central role in modern commander's battle plan. The factor of 'time' promises to envelope the dimensions of war as a force multiplier. The side that controls 'time' will be in superior position to conduct war in all dimensions.

28. **Myth 3: NCW applies only to large scale conflict with a peer competitor.** One might be tempted to reach this conclusion especially when viewing its applicability in Operations other than War (OOTW). This limitation is supported by the current state of development especially in the collection and analysis of appropriate information in such an operational environment. But even in such cases where the information is far less than perfect, it could be argued that being able to have a shared understanding of what is known and what is not known would be preferable to a situation in which units are operating in isolated ignorance. The enemy may be better at concealment than you are at finding him but the existence of the network will still make it easier for you to respond once he has engaged you. Despite the enormous benefits of using a network, it would be a folly to lose sight of the fact that it is still merely a tool to aid the commander in understanding and decision-making.

29. **Myth 4. NCW make it more vulnerable to Information Warfare (IW) and Asymmetric Attacks.** An associate attribute of NCW is on the going 'Revolution in Military Affairs (RMA)', highlighting the way in which enabling technologies such as intelligence, surveillance, command and control, simulation and training are fused together in information dominance and precision strike. Advocates of NCW also highlight the need of holistic amalgam of concepts of operations, command and control approaches, organizational forms, doctrine, force structure, support services and the like working together to leverage injection of technology—to what Admiral Owens of the US refers to as 'System of Systems'. This increasing dependence on such complex 'system of systems' also creates its own sets of vulnerabilities, especially in the realm of IW and its close linkage to asymmetric attacks wherein the weak resort to the use of technology against technology. Such a threat is about theft of secrets; it is about turning information against its owners and ultimately it is about denying the adversary the ability to use both his technology and information. It is

just that one cannot harness the distributed intelligence if the information content is diverted or tampered or even destroyed. Information networks have also created a tunnel to the centre of one's vulnerability, which can be exploited by any nation or collective effort of individuals at their discretion. And, with any extremely successful instrument, simple dependence could turn catastrophic if the enemy discovers a way of disabling the tool. Such vulnerabilities need to be fully examined as we operationalize the NCW concept.

30. **Myth 5. NCW would lift the proverbial 'fog' and 'friction' in warfare.** NCW by the virtue of its claim of 'Information superiority' leads to enhance 'Situational and Shared Awareness' and the resultant increases 'Speed of Command' and consequent 'Decision Superiority'. The ability to hit many high value targets simultaneously allows the employment of strategy of 'shock and awe' that will bring a situation to conclusion far more rapidly that attrition based approach. Clausewitz's image of 'fog' describes the limit to knowledge imposed by the battlefield. NCW key enablers reconstitute this notion in a way that permits overwhelming information dominance over technologically inferior opponents. But strategy is eternal; the disadvantage can be coped with by choosing when and where to fight. Changing information availability also changes, but does not end the role of 'friction'. The down side of high technology is equally important: depending on complex devices that are extraneous to the actual job of destroying one's target increases the points of failure. On the other hand, technology when it works also creates increasing flexibility and effectiveness. Infantry trained in the use of night-vision or thermal–imaging equipment and continuously linked with combat communication systems could indeed exploit synergy to become a more effective fighting organism.

Conclusion

31. Projected future operating environments emphasize the decisive advantage conferred by superior information

management and knowledge dominance. They will be the key to operational success in the decades ahead. NCW is a natural consequence of advances in IT and is here to stay. The move to net-centricity is irresistible, inexorable and necessary. The limitations as it appears now, as also the potential vulnerabilities of NCW need to be identified early so that timely action can be taken to deny success to any opponent. Although the broad tapestry of NCW concept is still emerging, there is clear evidence that shift to network centric operations are well underway. Few of the shortcomings and myths that have been mentioned in the preceding paragraphs do contain the germ of valid concern. We may not find perfect answers, but we can begin by posing the right questions. These need to be given due consideration as we proceed into the future.

32. If history is a guide, surely the present endeavours in operationalizing NCW concepts are indeed momentous steps. The views of the skeptics do point to some risks at the implementation stage, but there is no doubt that if NCW is effectively implemented it will be a huge force multiplier. While the task will not be easy, it will prepare us to fight the emerging contours of warfare better. There is compelling evidence that supports the theory of NCW. NCW, in the long run, offers unprecedented promise to achieve long-sought-after capabilities. Progress has been made in developing an understanding of the basics of network centric concepts and their ability to contribute to mission success. However, applications to date of NCW theory have barely scratched the surface of what is possible. The encouraging sign is the early experimentation and trials and acquisitions have provided significant justification to continue investing in the further development of NCW as the cornerstone enabler of future combat forces.

Bibliography

1. Network Centric Warfare: An overview of Emerging Theory by John J Garstka, Joint Staff, Directorate for C4 Systems.

2. The Challenge and Promise of Network Centric Warfare by Mr. John Luddy, Adjunct Fellow, Lexington Institute, Feb 2005.

3. Network Centric Warfare—Creating a Decisive War fighting Advantage, Director Force Transformation, Office of the Secretary of Defence, US—(Winter 2003).

4. Network Centric Warfare—Developing and Leveraging Information Technology, by David S. Alberts, John J. Garstka, Frederick P. Stein—CCRP Publications, 2nd Edition (Revised).

5. Proceedings of a 'National Seminar on Infostructure for Network Centric Warfare, 25-26, May 2004, organized under the aegis of Army Headquarters (Directorate General of Signals) and Confederation of Indian Industry (CII).

6. Network Centric Warfare: Its Origin and Future by Vice Admiral Arthur K. Cebrowski, U.S. Navy, and John J. Garstka, U.S. Naval Institute Proceedings—2003.

* * *

8

Operations in the Jungles

*Brig Trigunesh Mukherjee, AVSM (Retd)**

"Luck comes easily to people who work hard"

A Thing of the Past ?

After the Second World War, one area that seems to have been neglected by all armies of the world is operations in jungle terrain. Whether it has been due to focus on mobile operations, air operations, development of weapons etc., it is difficult to pinpoint. Perhaps it is an amalgamation of all these and the reluctance on the part of Armies to get involved in slow operations where results are not easy to see and they are rarely quick. So you hardly ever, if at all, hear of seminars on Jungle Warfare. In fact, even the Indian Army's training publication on Jungle Warfare was reviewed/reprinted towards the end of the seventies. Surely, three decades should demand an update.

---

* Brig (Retd.) Trigunesh Mukherjee, AVSM, retired as ADG-NCC

Yet, most countries with sizable armies have fairly large tracts of jungle terrain. In India's context, while it is true that we don't have pure jungles on our borders with Pakistan and China (except in small patches) there are large areas of jungle where other operations need to be launched quite often. Whenever there is a need to take a re-look at some of the terrains, focus invariably reverts to linear obstacles or the desert or amphibious operations etc., and the "jungles" get avoided.

Environmentally speaking, it is very important to protect the jungles but to even do so they can't be left on their own. The national writ must run in these areas and that can't happen by isolation.

Why Now ?

In the Indian context, the jungles are being utilized by groups that do not have the strength to operate openly. In addition, they provide good infiltration routes and good areas to hide – be they weapons and equipment or people. Even if one cannot say jungles are where operations will take place in future it would not be out of place to say that a lot of irregular operations will take place in the jungles. Not giving due importance to operating in the jungles is proving quite expensive periodically when heavy casualties are incurred by the police forces. The security forces need to understand and utilize the jungles to their advantage and not get beaten by the insurgent or terrorist or a brigand like Veerappan. Unless the security forces are familiar with the jungles and operating in them they will not be able to "fight the guerilla like a guerilla" [credo of the Counter Insurgency and Jungle Warfare School].

The deployment for the United Nations also takes our forces to the jungles. If at any time the objective changes from "peace keeping" to "peace enforcing" we will be found wanting in our preparations.

An important point to remember for the powers that be is not to rely on previous information and knowledge.

Terrain has changed, communications have changed, people have changed, operations have changed etc, therefore, a fresh look is needed.

Geographical Areas to Look At

The Indian Army has always been aware of the areas that may prove to be trouble spots because of their systematic environment scanning. But these were perhaps never followed through because there always seemed to be more important aspects that demanded attention – strike formations, air operations, defending linear obstacles and so on. A strategy of avoidance seems to have been followed. Everyone is aware that familiarization, intelligence gathering and actual training for operations in the jungles would be tiresome, long drawn and unglamourous. Well, it is high time people dirtied their hands and came to terms with reality lest they get a bloody nose if they are ever drawn into operations in the jungle scenario.

The areas one can easily list are :

- **The Andaman & Nicobar Islands.** They are of strategic interest to all littoral states as also to states that want to "extend" power/influence like China and the United States. Because of the demographic pattern and distribution large areas are not even visited by the security forces, forget about extending influence. Here, the western side is treated as unapproachable but that is by us, do maritime infiltrators view it in a similar fashion? It may take a long time to discover infiltration and illegal settlements and even longer to get rid of them. Remember it is not that difficult to spread out specially in the bigger islands. In any case, the Chinese have Coco Islands already.
- **Sunderbans.** A rich and diverse but delicate ecological treasure house and in close proximity to a country that is overpopulated and somewhat discriminatory. Therefore, an easy choice to shift

habitat and upset both demographic and environmental balance.

- **Eastern States (with International Borders).** All are very susceptible to movement of people (be they people in search of livelihood or smugglers or poachers or terrorists or insurgents) as it is, because of our porous borders. Add to this the advantage of jungles which exist in great expanses. The thought that we may not even be aware of the magnitude of the problem and reality is frightening. The only silver lining, if one can call it one, is that ideology transfer is not so common.
- **Regions with Extremist Influence.** Currently they may be Maoist/Naxal oriented but that may change without changing the advantages of being in these areas. They are remote and mostly in the proximity of, if not in, the jungles. Depending on the influence they wield and their capacity to escalate matters, the areas will demand intervention by security forces including the army. The very spread is worrisome – Bengal, Bihar, Jharkhand, Orissa, Madhya Pradesh, Chhattisgarh and Andhra Pradesh. And it does not mean the other areas are free from such leanings – Maharashtra (advantage of access to the sea and hills), Kerala, Karnataka, Tamil Nadu (with pronounced sympathies for the LTTE) – and they all have a lot of jungle area.
- **Jammu and Kashmir.** Since the forests (not really jungles) here can't provide enough natural food they will mainly be used for movement and temporary stays.

With that spread of likely jungle based threat areas, it would seem prudent to give the subject of operations in the jungles, some importance and thought.

Some Characteristics of Jungles

While a general idea exists in people's minds it is important for the Army and other security forces to understand the jungles really well. In fact, make friends with the terrain. The best way, no doubt, is to spend time in the jungles (all types because there are a lot of differences) but mental preparation can start early. Some of the more important points to look at are :

- **Physical and Mental Fitness.** Very often energy is easily sapped in the jungles, therefore, one has to have the physical abilities to overcome these effects. Added to this are the feelings of loneliness and blindness (because one cannot see far off). Robustness of the mind is critical for operations in these areas. Sometimes, the fact that you cannot see the sky can upset people in unpredictable ways.

- **Flora and Fauna.** Familiarity with the flora and fauna will help immensely in making people comfortable in the jungles. Knowledge about leeches, snakes, insects, animals etc., as well as undergrowth, root formation, water yielding plants etc., need to be mastered.

- **6 Senses.** More than anywhere else, the need to develop the 6 senses is very pronounced in the jungles. The five basic senses are used much more in this environment. One needs to add on the 6th Sense and intuition because clear pictures are very rare. The training can commence anywhere but will have to be honed once one is in the jungle environment.

- **Stress.** Getting familiar with stress and finding one's own ways of relieving stress is even more important in the jungles. One can add fatigue to this and look at a more rounded solution.

- **Lack of accurate Maps.** Maps will not be easily available and accurate ones may not exist. People have to quickly assess accuracy and make their own maps. If thermal imaging is available then it would improve matters but then one has to have some people trained in interpreting thermal images. Rather than complaining of "lack of maps" one must quickly understand how to work with available information and knowledge. If available, tourist maps, trekkers' maps, garden surveys, oil surveys etc., should be fully used.

- **Use of Weapons etc.** Close proximity weapons with high accuracy would be the rule and longer range weapons, the exception. Weapons that do not jam and can fire at a fairly high speed would be essential.
- **Surveillance Systems.** Though one will have to depend on one's own (human) surveillance skills, advantage must be taken of unobtrusive and light surveillance systems that are currently available. Any additional warning will be critical to the soldier in the jungle.

A Few Operational Aspects

All the basics, of course, hold good but in the jungle environment there are some more important aspects. One, sustained operations in the true sense – regaining contact once it is lost, is virtually impossible. Therefore, once contact is established operations must be pressed to its logical conclusion. Two focus – it is very easy to lose focus because so many things will seem to be happening at the same time. Three, capacity to continue operations even if communications fail. Four, be prepared for surprises – a lot of "what if" training is essential. Five, have to develop tolerance for ambiguity (not just the leaders) because things will rarely be black and white clear. Six, leaders must be well versed in operating in an environment of uncertainty. Seven, thorough and meticulous planning with flexibility to accept changes. Last but not the least, people must develop the capacity to rest whenever possible – fatigue takes a big toll in the jungles.

Comparative Surveillance. Since our remote sensing and thermal imaging facilities are quite advanced they must help the soldier on the ground. Time separated comparative surveillance, results will give a much clearer real time idea to forces about how things are changing around them and that will enable preparation and decision making.

Support Operations

Needless to say, all support operations, be they fire support, movement support, replenishment, casualty evacuation etc., must be planned in detail and executed with intent to succeed. Operating in the jungles is lonely enough by itself so troops can well do without the feeling that support is sluggish or worse, uninterested.

Points Not Addressed

Since features of dealing with insurgents or terrorists are fairly well documented and very well known to the Indian Army they are not being touched upon. The intention here has been to focus only on operations in the jungles. All aspects of dealing with an insurgent threat will hold in terms of knowledge, study of habits etc. It is also not the intention to focus separately on each type of jungle – our jungles differ quite a lot from area to area.

Where Do We Go Next ?

To start with, the Army (and the other security forces) needs to stop neglecting operations in the jungles in its thinking. If one analyses the curricula (what is implemented NOT what is planned) of schools of instruction, or the training events of formations, or emphasis in units it will be quite clear that JUNGLES don't feature. This is possibly due to lack of interest and (perhaps sadly) because of lack of glamour appeal. After all how does a commander showcase something in the "jungle"?

Some immediate attention is needed to develop a practical doctrine. Once this is formulated and features in training directives "operations in the jungles" will get its due importance. One must not forget that the Indian Army gets its training very professionally and in depth, so there is no reason for it, not to bring jungles within its focus. The publication, "Jungle Warfare" perhaps needs to be replaced (quickly and not with a long gestation period) by "Operations in the Jungles", because "warfare" seems to be definitely out now. Visits and stays in various jungles would be quite easy to organize for the Army and the impact will be outstanding. Jungles cannot be learnt theoretically.

The earlier we focus on operations in the jungles the easier it will be for the Army to operate in such terrain with ease and effectiveness. One has to accept that the need may arise at any time for security forces to be deployed in jungle terrain and the better prepared they are, easier the operations will be.

* * *

9

Preparing for Next World War: Future Weapons Technologies

*Dr Shivathanu Pillai, DRDO**

1. World War I was the outcome of political brinkmanship of world's leading powers motivated by rampant nationalism, economic expansion, and pursuit of military prestige. The nationalism was fuelled by the dangerous belief that one race is superior to another. The great European powers embarked on an arms race that ran in tandem with the scramble for colonies. The need to protect far flung colonies and the lust for gaining military advantage in often shifting alliances with Britain, Germany, Russia, and France being in the center stage created conditions for the world war. The events between August 1914 to November 1918 brought about unparalleled destruction and loss of life giving birth to new political geography and creation of an international body to monitor conduct of international affairs.

* Dr Shivathanu Pillai, DRDO is with the BRAHMOS

2. World War I created conditions for World War II. Cornered and helpless Germany sparked ideal environment for a dangerously ambitious dictator Adolf Hitler along with fascist Mussolini of Italy and victorious Japan to start the most destructive conflict in the history of mankind, leaving an estimated 15 million military and 34 million civilians dead. The end of World War II ushered in the nuclear age and commencement of Cold War dominated the world events. Decolonalisation and creation of United Nations followed.

3. Today after 62 years:

(a) On one hand globalization has brought countries of different continents together strengthening the economic ties, reducing social and cultural differences, while on the other the extremism and non-tolerance for each other's religious sentiments has become the biggest ever threat to the world peace. In the words of the former Israel's spy chief. "We are in the midst of World War III. A person walks through the streets of Tel Aviv, Barcelona, and Buenos Aires and doesn't sense that there is a war going on but there are deadly terrorist attacks in Madrid, London, and New York".

(b) The Cold War seems to surface again seeking refuse of variety of avoidable causes. The Uni-polar world created by disintegration of erstwhile USSR is taking shape of multi-polarity with latent ambitions of few powerful nations surfacing slowly but dangerously.

(c) The growing demands for energy and the need to save nation's integral energy resources are hinting at situation where "survival of fittest" theory fits well leading to ambitions growing un-proportionately bigger beyond all the gravitational limitations of earth extending to space. The claims on resources have also been made for extreme regions of world including Arctic, Antarctic. Efforts are on to create boundaries under sub-sea in international waters.

(d) Stock piling of arms including nuclear warheads has become routine national objectives even for developing countries. The developed countries have already crossed the threshold of stock piling years before. A recent incident of USA where one B-52 bomber took off with six nuclear tipped missiles on cross country flight unnoticed, substantiates this fact.

4. The religious fundamentalism coupled with fight for energy seem more likely reason for triggering the World War III which will be different from previous wars in many ways. The technology driven war if not curtailed will ultimately be aimed at complete destruction of adversary's fighting potential of all forms. The war will be characterized by: -

(a) Formation of military alliance between friendly countries.

(b) Use of high-end technology driven war machinery.

(c) Spread of war over the entire globe where selection of ground of own choosing for fighting war will seldom be available.

(d) Fighting in all four plains namely surface, sea, air, and space.

(e) Precision attacks will be preferred over mass destruction till such time situations remain under control.

(f) Electronic warfare will dominate the war scenario.

(g) Supremacy in space, air and sea will pave the way for ground forces to ultimately seize the land mass though initially there will be limited role of ground forces as compared to the previous wars.

(h) The danger of any rogue nation/terrorist outfit using weapons of mass destruction will always haunt the world community.

(i) In the event of war getting out of hands, the use of massive nuclear force with a view to completely annihilates the adversary will be resorted to. In that case the nation having inbuilt survivability and preparedness to operate in nuclear environment with ability of massive retaliation is likely to prevail.

Preparing for World War III

5. Any nation to survive the next world war will presumably require following capabilities: -

(a) To fight a multi-directional, multi-layered and asymmetric non-linear war.

(b) Possess capabilities to maintain lasting air and sea supremacy along with the option of space dominance.

(c) Capability to contain adversary and survive nuclear attacks without losing strike capability.

(d) Undertake massive retaliation to render adversary incapable of fighting war.

6. In order to possess such capabilities a nation needs to have: -

(a) Strong national will, backed by trustworthy and strong alliance without compromising national integrity.

(b) Modern defense forces backed by reliable logistic infrastructure.

(c) Preparation of national civilian industries for switching over to defense production, if situation so demands.

(d) Preparation of civilian population, townships and communication centres to survive the nuclear environment.

(e) Maintain strong nuclear force at all levels i.e. surface, air, sea, and sub-sea capable of surviving and undertaking massive assured retaliation.

(f) Seamless coordination between air, ground, and sea based forces to ensure synergy of operations making maximum use of resources based on real time information driven command and control system.

(g) Capability to switch large size forces from different theatres to point of application, alternatively, in a network centric warfare concentrate required weight without physically moving the forces.

Future War Technologies

7. Technology, in its all possible dimensions, affects warfare in all plains i.e. land, air, sea, and space. The famous British General and Military thinker John Fuller stated, "Victory in war depends 99 percent on high technology and one percent on other factors". 1982 Arab Israel War amply demonstrated the same. Technologies that are expected to be used in next world war, though dynamic, are distinct and have laudable bearing on each other.

Space Technologies

8. Space operations include space control, force enhancement, space support and force application. These are achieved by variety of satellites and/or space platforms that have either been developed or are under development.

9. In the next war use of satellites both in passive and active mode will be prominent. Apart from working as a global eye in the space, satellites will also work as weapon platforms using array of sensors.

10. Variety of satellite constellations along with the number of task specific satellites and micro-satellites will provide enormous capabilities to defense forces in next war. Some of these are: -

(a) Navigational aid.

(b) Fix location of own weapon platforms and movement of adversary's weapons and war machinery using high precision afocal photometric telescope equal to quality of simulated imagery and SARLupe radar reconnaissance system with one meter resolution.

(c) Missile guidance and multi-layered missile defense shield.

(d) Serve as communication hub for passage of data and provide inter-connectivity between 'sensor and shooter' using high power 'C' and 'Ku' band communication links.

(e) Conduct of post-flight analysis.

(f) Undertake space control operations to provide freedom of action in space for friendly forces while, when directed, deny it to an adversary. Provide combat commanders the ability to undertake counter communication, counter surveillance and reconnaissance functions.

(g) Gain and maintain space superiority through counter space operations having defensive and offensive elements to achieve variety of affects from temporary denial to complete destruction of adversary's space capabilities.

(h) Carry out destruction with 'Hypervelocity Rod Bundles' of ground targets anywhere in the world from space. May include strafing and bombing from space, in times to come.

(i) Space based infrared systems gather information about activities relating to strategic and tactical missiles in the world.

11. Offensive counter space technologies are: -

(a) **Missiles.** Employed against a variety of space capabilities of adversary including launch facilities, ground stations and space nodes.

(b) **Anti-Satellite Weapons.** These are direct ascent and co-orbital systems that employ various mechanisms to destroy an on-orbit spacecraft.

(c) **Directed Energy Weapons.** These weapons are capable of wide range of affects against on-orbit spacecraft including heating, blinding optics, degradation and destruction. Some of these are Thunderball, Airborne Laser, Tactical high energy Laser, MIRACL, HELEX and Space based Lasers.

(d) Counter space systems that deny use of satellite imagery with reversible non-damaging effects.

12. Simultaneous efforts are also on to remove space debris with the help of high power/energy Lasers to ensure collision free operations in the space.

Air Based Technologies

13. Air power has always been the prime force in creating conditions favourable to ground forces. The modern operational concept revolves around effect oriented operations rather than platform and weapon dependency. The key features around which technologies revolve are knowledge (intelligence, surveillance and reconnaissance), speed, precision and lethality.

14. In addition to the technologies that are already in use, the host of new technologies will dominate the next war. These are: -

(a) New generation aircrafts with advanced avionics suite and cabins having equal capabilities for both 'air to air' and 'air to ground' missions with high agility, wide operational altitude-speed envelope and supersonic cruise mode. The onboard precision guided weapons will work as 'effectors' in an integrated net-centric force and availability of intelligence will result in enhanced autonomous cooperative engagement. These will also have radar contrast guidance ensuring jamming avoidance. Smart precision guided bombs, guided missiles and air defense missiles to kill adversary ballistic missiles will form part of these multi-role aircrafts.

(b) Attack helicopter with situational awareness kit, synthetic vision, electronic flight bag charts to display charts and manuals, real time weather graphics and terrain awareness warning systems will spearhead the attack launched by ground forces. Modern helicopter with fire and forget capabilities will ensure avoidance of danger zone. These will have optronic system with two channel Laser designator-range finder and supersonic missiles having capabilities of investigation, detection, tracking and target illumination. Helicopters will also have capabilities to deploy chaff and flare counter measures to deflect missiles with the help of missile warning system and radar warning receivers.

(c) 'High Energy Solid State Laser System' on board air platforms to provide satellite kill capability.

(d) Target acquisition and designation with day-night all weather sights.

(e) Improved identification friend and foe technology.

(f) Signal intelligence and network attack aircrafts with radar jamming radars.

(g) Sky air traffic management systems.

(h) Close air support aircraft have precision navigation and targeting system with liquid crystal multi-functional display and wide angle head-up display.

(i) 'Focused Lethality Munitions' to include low collateral damage bombs with GPS or Laser guidance kit and moving target weapons.

(j) Stand-off land attack missile operating in 'L' band spectrum.

(k) Drones and UAVs with 'Ground Situational Awareness Kit' and shoot spotter gun fire acquisition system.

(l) 'Air to ground' and radar guided 'air to air' missiles.

(m) Military transport helicopter with 10 to 30 metric tonne capability.

(n) 'Air to air' refuelling delivering upto 900 gallons per minute.

(o) Adaptive versatile engine technology ensuring optimized performance over a broad range of altitude and speed.

(p) Satellite telecommunication adapter and ground based switching unit to allow use of variety of satellites of different standards.

(q) Multi-carrier based Airborne Early Warning Systems.

(r) Ramjet powered beyond visual range 'air to air' missiles.

Land Based Technologies

15. The quest for making battlefield more transparent to each soldier and his chain of command has given birth to host of new technologies that will make the future soldier more intelligent and responsive. Rapid access to product and services, technology insertion, system integration, system engineering, software development and logistic support has made battlefield more dynamic.

16. Extensive use of weapons utilizing sensors and robotics with improved close combat capabilities completing sensor to shooter loop for every soldier with tactical intranet geographic dissemination in real time for information management, will be common in next war.

17. The future soldier will be state-of-the-art self contained, compact fighting machine with visual chemical and biological sensors, miniaturized communication and GPS systems, Laser guided weapons with hand held computer displaying and video links. Each fighting entity will have integral rocket launchers, automatic grenade launchers, anti-material bunker bursting rifles, flame throwers, bio-sensors,

hand held thermal images, advanced frequency hopping radio sets ensuring better lethality, survivability, mobility and sustainment. Bio-sensors will serve as life sign detection, decision support and trauma assessment systems.

18. Major technologies being provided under 'Improved Operational Soldier System' are: -

(a) Sniping system with light reticule.

(b) Thermal sniping system.

(c) Laser telemeter.

(d) Interface with helmet mounted display.

(e) Enhanced precision of the aiming systems.

(f) Enhanced efficiency ammunition.

(g) Integrated GPS navigation systems.

(h) Logistics and functional support vehicle.

(i) Micro computers with LCD display.

(j) Ballistic and NBC protection systems including gas mask.

(k) Reduced signature suites.

19. The other land based cutting edge technologies that will tilt the balance in conventional war scenario are: -

(a) Tactical precision guided weapon systems including guided rockets and cruise missiles.

(b) Intelligence, surveillance and reconnaissance sensors and data exploitation systems using synthetic aperture radar, still and motion electro optical/infrared imagery and electronic support measure sensors to improve situational awareness of commanders.

(c) Multi-layered protection from air attacks using active and passive measures and precision guided air defense missiles.

(d) Bio-metric technologies to recognize a person based on psychological and behavioural characteristics and provide highly secure identification and personal verification solutions consisting of both hardware and software.

(e) Future Combat Systems based on variety of unmanned ground and aerial vehicles using robotics will provide advanced network air and ground manoeuvr capability. The highlights of the technologies are: -

(i) Hybrid electric drive engine.

(ii) Close combat armament systems.

(iii) Sensors.

(iv) Active protection systems.

(v) High voltage batteries.

(vi) Signature reduction material.

(f) Active armour defeating all types of anti-tank guided missile systems at a significant distance. Tracked and wheeled vehicles for mobile rapid action forces with a balance between need for force protection and strategic deployment, acting as main land strike force, will use following technologies: -

(i) Protected mobility and equipment support.

(ii) Enhanced armour support.

(iii) Chemical, biological, radiological and nuclear reconnaissance.

(iv) Remotely delivered/distributed mines systems.

(v) Obstacle crossing, bridge laying and mine bursting systems.

(vi) Mobile mortar platforms, UAV carriers and radar platforms.

(g) Integral task oriented drones, UAVs and micro UAVs for variety of applications.

(h) Laser to assess range, weather, wind conditions and for better fire control solutions.

(i) Night vision devices based on imaging infrared/un-cooled infrared/Mercury Cadmium Telluride (MCT) detectors and biometric thermal images providing full vision in total darkness.

(j) Modern data network with ability to track units/individuals in real time in areas which do not have GPS coverage using radio communicators, sustaining voice, video and data links, inertial and magnetic systems offering continuous position tracking.

Sea Based Technologies

20. Countries all over the world have tailor made naval forces based on their geographical locations and national ambitions. Naval forces will play major role in next war like previous wars. With introduction of satellites, long range precision guided weapons housed in sea platforms/sub-sea platforms with improved communication systems, stealth technologies and integrated command and control technologies, the role of navy has entered a new paradigm. Moving from steam propelled platforms to modern propulsion techniques such as gas turbine, diesel engine and hybrid combinations (combined gas and gas/diesel electric systems/combined diesel or gas turbine/combined diesel and diesel/combined diesel electric and gas turbine), nuclear propulsion and water-jet propulsion, the naval warfare has become swift, concealed and globalized. Next war will see improved cruisers, destroyers, frigates, corvettes, petrol gunboats, mine layers and mine sweepers, sloops, landing crafts, guided missile cruisers, aircraft carriers, submarines both conventional (diesel electric/fuel cell-powered) and nuclear powered which will change the dimensions of sea warfare when compared to previous wars.

21. The major sea based technologies that the next war will witness are: -

(a) Long range high speed precision anti-ship missiles with multi-target attack capability.

(b) Electro-optical tracking and fire control systems for target detection and tracking.

(c) Long range surveillance and reconnaissance systems with improved image gathering providing in better common situational understanding.

(d) Radars to perform non-cooperative recognition based on target's kinematics behaviour, doppler spectrum and high resolution range/inverse synthetic aperture radar image.

(e) New ship building technologies for mine sweeping and mine hunting with extremely reduced signatures and enhanced seek resistance.

(f) Operation of unmanned water vehicles from parent submarine with reliable acoustic or radio frequency links creating local area network.

(g) Deployment of submarines and ship based hard kill (long/short range missiles) and soft kill (electronic warfare and decoys) systems.

(h) Employment of "fast crafts" of 60-70 knots speed with reduced radar signatures, very high manoeuverability, acceleration, outstanding seakeeping, high performance in rough waters and limited "G" force for crew and equipment.

(i) Chemical detection equipment.

(j) High power RF systems with high power microwave or ultrawide band systems to overwhelm the ability of the target to reject or disperse RF energy leaving the incoming missiles susceptible to disruption or destruction.

(k) Stealth non-nuclear, network enabled submarine with advance propulsion technologies, new geometrics of hull coatings, rudders and propellers, suppressed underwater electrical and magnetic potentials, new sensors and weapons.

(l) Surface to underwater guided weapons, Super-cavitating Torpedoes Advanced mines (combined Influence mines, Morred mines, Encapsulated mines, Tethered mines).

(m) Anti-missile.

(n) Advanced Gun propulsion concepts (electro magnetic gun, light gas gun, ram accelerator gun, electro thermal gun, liquid propelled gun and advanced solid propelled gun).

(o) Advanced maritime unmanned aerial vehicles with vertical takeoff and landing, unmanned combat air vehicle, unmanned search system and multi-mission reconfigurable unmanned underwater vehicle.

(p) Stealth technologies reducing radar, acoustic, magnetic, electric and infrared signatures, making the ship nearly invisible to adversary's sensors.

(q) Platforms for multi-mission maritime surveillance and control.

(r) Electronic warfare, networking and advanced radars to achieve electronic attack (kinetic and non-kinetic fires) and linking of ground forces to maritime forces.

22. The future technologies are likely to be dominated by Micro Electro Mechanical Systems and Nanotechnology, Laser technology, cyber war related technologies, space based technologies including Directed Energy Weapons, High power microwave weapons, charged particle beam weapons and Electronic warfare, counter and countermeasure technologies. World will continue to develop new war machines and weapons of mass destruction however, reliance on technology alone may not yield the desired results. The world is bound to witness mass destruction by the hands of few politically unstable and socially disturbed nations whose

ideologies are based on religious fundamentalism. The preparation for use of nuclear bombs by Pakistan against India during Kargil war is an example of the same. The real victory will come to the nation which prepares itself to survive through nuclear attacks while retaining multi-level assured retaliation capability.

* * *

10

Pakistan's Intelligence: Present & Future

MALOY KRISHNA DHAR, IPS (RETD)

Some sensible and humourous Pakistani friends say: every country has an army; in Pakistan, the Army has a country. In most countries, the people own everything; in Pakistan, everything is owned by the Army.

This comment does not require elaboration as history of Pakistan proves beyond doubt that the Armed Forces and their ancillary tentacles have permanently hijacked the country. Alongwith the country, the Army has hijacked every tool of governance, including its intelligence agencies. The civil society's malarial shivers for democracy are graciously allowed to wear a quilt of popular mandate either under extreme local exigencies or under foreign

---

* Maloy Krishna Dhar, IPS (Retd) is former Joint Director of Indian Intelligence Bureau and a specialist on Pakistan and Jihad related matters.

pressure. Democracy was somewhat restored after Pakistan suffered reverses in East Pakistan in 1971. Other interludes apart, this time around, the United States has forced the military ruler to try a mix of democratic and military weapons against the Taliban, Al Qaeda and several home grown jihadi tanzeems. Pakistan Army and intelligence apparatus either have failed or have lost the appetite to fight the Islamist forces. The fearful civilians shiver precariously between a blundering Army and the advancing jihadis.

Democracy is treated as external facades of the Pakistani polity. The kernel of power is hidden in the Armed Forces and the Intelligence Services of Pakistan. These two complementary pillars of anti-people establishment of Pakistan are buttressed by the huge arrays of retired officers of the Armed Forces occupying innumerable (over 500) administrative, managerial and diplomatic posts. The professional civil servants and puppet political leaders belong to the lowest rung of the establishment machineries that run the country. They exist because they are yet to be extinct.

The Armed Forces have adopted a creed that it is the permanent political spine of Pakistan and its intelligence services; especially the Inter Services Intelligence (ISI) is the important stabilising radar. Though an integral part of the Army Establishment, the ISI, managed by the Ministry of Defence, is not the only intelligence agency of Pakistan.

The major Intelligence security agencies of Pakistan are:

Federal Intelligence Agencies:

i. Intelligence Bureau

ii. Ehtasab (National Accountability) Bureau

Ministry of Defence:

i. Inter Services Intelligence

ii. Inter Services Public Relations

Army:

i. Military Intelligence

ii. Special Services Group

iii. Surveyor General of Pakistan (Geographical Division)

Ministry of Interior:

i. Federal Investigation Agency

ii. Narcotics Control Division.

It is not necessary to narrate details of all these of Pakistan's intelligence and security Administration.

Besides the Intelligence Bureau, the Ehtasab Bureau (National Accountability Bureau), Federal Investigation Agency and the Narcotic Control Division play important roles in domestic intelligence and security administration.

The Intelligence Bureau headed by Brig (Retd) Ijaz Ahmad Shah, a confidant and former ISI handler of Afghan Mujahideen and Osama bin Laden had earned enough notoriety in recent times. He was named before and after arrival of Benazir Bhutto as one of the officials who opposed any concession to the democratic forces. Such controversy around the IB is not new. However, after the elected government took over in 2008 Ahmad Shah resigned. He was replaced by Dr. Shoaib Suddle, a former IGP of Sind.

Pakistan Intelligence Bureau (PIB) is the inheritor of the Central Intelligence Bureau of British India. Its counterpart, the Intelligence Bureau of India, is the prime internal security and intelligence agency of the government of India. The Intelligence Bureau, one of the oldest security and intelligence edifices of the British Empire, had inherited the established skills and tools of the trade. Prior to 1958 military takeover, the PIB used to be answerable to the Cabinet Division of the Prime Minister's secretariat. The PIB, like its Indian counterpart, covers activities of the political parties, activists and carries out internal security related functions, which encompass the entire panorama of the civil society and internal functioning of the Jihadi tanzeems. It is also responsible for counter-intelligence operations on Pakistani soil.

The Intelligence Bureau had gained prominence under Benazir Bhutto's last tenure. She used the agency and its controversial Director Masood Sharif to topple provincial governments and to carry out extensive surveillance on her political opponents and adversaries. Such blatant use of the IB to the consternation of the military and the ISI was cited as one of the reasons for Benazir's dismissal in November 1996. However, under President Musharraf the IB attained greater prominence as 'terrorist liaison' and 'trouble shooting' operators.

Organisationally, Pakistan's IB follows the old British pattern, which is also the beaten path for the Indian Intelligence Bureau. It has strong presence in the provinces with units located at *tehsil* (revenue unit) and sub divisional level. The IB has significant presence on the international borders with India and Afghanistan. It shares over 25 units with the ISI in Balochistan where a separatist battle is shaking Pakistan.

In certain sensitive operational areas like the Indian borders, NWFP, Northern Areas, the ISI, Narcotics Bureau, MI Directorate and the Geographical Division also share joint responsibilities with the IB. In Gilgit and Baltistan areas, the IB shares its responsibility with the Special Services Group (SSG).

The last IB chief has had a colourful career in the army. As an experienced hand of the Afghanistan Bureau of the ISI, he handled Mullah Omar, the Taliban Chief and Osama bin Laden, the Al Qaeda supremo. His friendship with Gulbuddin Hikmatyar is legendary. Even now, Hikmatyar's camps in Peshawar are patronised by the IB. Brig. Ijaz had prominently figured in the internationally infamous Mukhtaran Mai case. He had tried to suppress the case under orders from his boss Musharraf.

There are reliable information of his open connectivity with Mohammad Atta and Ahmed Omar Sheikh, related to 9/11 attack on the USA and Daniel Pearl murder. Musharraf had tried to accommodate his loyal soldier by offering him appointment as High Commissioner to Australia and Ambassador to Indonesia. Both the governments had spurned the posting on grounds of Brigadier Ijaz Ahmad Shah's alleged connectivity with Lashkar-e-Toiba and Jaish-e-Mohammad.

The attack on Benazir Bhutto's motorcade by two alleged Al Qaeda suicide bombers has drawn instant criticism from the former PM of Pakistan and a section of the media. Brigadier Ijaz now lives in Australia.

The other important intelligence agency of Pakistan that has gained global eminence is the Inter Services Intelligence (ISI). The Inter Services Intelligence Directorate was conceived, way back in 1948, apparently as a nucleus inter-services co-ordination module and a tool to generate external intelligence, by Major General R. Cawthorne, an Australia born British Army officer, who had opted for the Pakistan Army and served as the Deputy Chief of Staff of Pakistan Army.

Though the credit is given to Cawthorne, the inspiration had come from Britain. Pakistan army had inherited a Military Intelligence unit and did not require a special agency to coordinate different wings of the infant armed forces. Pakistan was also not positioned as a global player to take up a crash programme for creating an external intelligence agency like the MI6 and the CIA. At the initial stage of transfer of power, Britain needed the ISI as a companion agency to strengthen its own strategic perspectives in the region. They were keen to use this agency as a watchtower against Afghanistan, Russia and China. The British HQ also wanted the ISI for keeping a watch on the new corps of Pakistani Army officers.

However, after hijacking the democratic dispensation Pakistan army did not strictly follow the British blueprint.

Pakistan drifted closer to the USA, which had emerged as the greatest surviving power after the Second World War. With the initiation of the Cold War, Pakistan was drawn to the US led coalition and security umbrellas floated by the anti-Soviet countries. The ISI, thereafter, leapfrogged to international area as a partner agency of the CIA and MI6.

Besides fulfilling its commitments to the US headed global intelligence and security tasking the ISI was extensively used as back as in 1958-60 to foment ethnic unrest in Northeast India and Kashmir. Gradually the ISI emerged as the main 'proxy war' tool of Pakistan against India, which it fought through conventional intelligence operations, direct involvement, operations through jihadi tanzeems patronised by the State and through third country operations. The sordid story is an integral part of Indo-Pak relations spanning 50 years of Pakistani 'proxy war' against India encompassing Kashmir, Punjab, Northeast and hinterland operations.

It is necessary to understand the basic structure of the evil machine of Pakistan that had played decisive roles in collaboration with the Royal Saudi Intelligence, MI6 and the CIA in defeating the Cold War enemy of the West in the Communist Vietnam or Afghanistan. It also played significant roles in the rise of the Taliban, Al Qaeda and Islamist terrorism almost everywhere in the world. Footprints of the jihadist activities anywhere in the world finally lead to the soil of Pakistan.

Following is the available list of illustrious heads of the ISI who had fashioned the political characters of the army, dominated its political spectrum and carried out open and secret wars against its historical enemy India and enemies of its Western allies.

1. Brig. Riazat Hussain — 1958 onwards.
2. Lt.Gen. Ghulam Jillani Khan — 1969 to early years of Zia-ul-Haq.
3. Lt.Gen. Akhtar Abdur Rahman — Zia regime till March 1987.

4. Lt.Gen. Hamid Gul	March '87-May 1989.
5. Lt.Gen. (Retd) Shamsur Rahman Kallue	May '89-Aug 1990.
6. Maj. General Assad Durrani	Aug '90-March 1992.
7. Lt.Gen. Javed Nasir	March'92-May 1993.
8. Lt.Gen. Javed Ashraf Kazi	May'93-June 1994.
9. Lt.Gen. Nasim Raja	June'94-1996.
10. Lt.Gen. Ziauddin	1996—sacked by Musharraf in 1999. His retirement benefits were reportedly denied.
11. Lt.Gen. Mahmood Ahmad	Dismissed by Musharraf under American pressure for complicity with the 9/11 conspirators. India, it is reported, had supplied supporting material to the USA.
12. Lt. Gen Ehsan-ul-Haq	Posted on Oct 8, 2001. He was the Corps Commander at Peshawar. He was formerly posted at Pakistan High Commission in Delhi in the rank of Counsellor. Removed in October 2004.
13. Lt.Gen. Ashfaq Kiyani	Appointed on October 4, 2004, now Army Chief.
14. Lt. Gen. Nadeem Taj	Appointed on September 20, 2007.

General Nadeem is a fierce Musharraf loyalist, he is a staunch Punjabi Jat from Jhelum area and is related to him through his wife. He had been his Military Secretary and was in the same flight from Colombo when Musharraf was being stopped from landing by the then PM Nawaz Sharif and after a brief coup. General Nadeem enjoyed complete trust of Musharraf.

Following is the broad divisions of the functional structure of the ISI:

1. Joint Counter-Intelligence Bureau (JCIB) — it is responsible for counter-intelligence activities and operations;
2. Joint Intelligence Signal Bureau (JISB) — it generates and denies Signal intelligence and liaise with the Signal Corps of the Armed Forces and the US and UK signal intelligence community;
3. Joint Intelligence Bureau (JIB) — it handles political matters. One section is assigned to study and assess Indian political developments;
4. Joint Intelligence Finance (JIF) — it manages budgetary and non-budgetary funds of the ISI; evaluates and approves critical operations;
5. Joint Intelligence Technical (JIT) — it is responsible for technical, including ElInt, PhotoInt, ImageInt, SatInt, etc;
6. Joint Arms Direction Group (JADG)—this wing is responsible for planning coordination in military exercises and procurement of weapons from unconventional sources, besides periodical evaluation of joint exercises;
7. Joint Intelligence Miscellaneous (JIM) — it oversees forward intelligence tasks, sabotage and subversion operations in foreign countries. Three sections are devoted to India;
8. Joint Intelligence North (JIN) — it is the hub of operations in Kashmir and other "special operations";
9. Foreign Liaison Section (FLS) — responsible for liaison with friendly foreign intelligence services;
10. Inter Services Federal Intelligence (ISFI) — it supplements the intelligence efforts of the provincial governments and often works as the direct arm of

the political/military bosses in internal political matters;

11. Public and Service Groups (P&SG) — it functions in close liaison with the Joint Chiefs of Staff Committee and maintains media liaison. The post-holder is generally close to the Chief of the Army Staff and the top executive. The position holder is handpicked;
12. Joint Intelligence X — its exact functional charter is not known. It is said that this wing is responsible for Intelligence Estimate, Threat Assessment and Formulation of Highly Sensitive Operations, including assassination, in collaboration with the JIB, JIM, JIN and ISFI.

Like most other intelligence organisations, the ISI has put in position a well-defined functional and operational structure as follows:

Director General Intelligence (DG ISI)

(Three star General)

•

Deputy Director General—Political

(Two star officer)

•

Deputy Director General—External I

(Two star officer)

•

Deputy Director General—External II

(Two star officer)

The number of two star officers has proliferated over the years and it is estimated that four such officers of the rank of Major General (one each from the Air Force and Navy) have been put incharge of designated divisions. These are reported to be post-Nawaz Sharif developments.

The DDG (Pol) controls the territorial and subject desks and sections, which cover the activities of the political parties, student, labour, mujahideen organisations, madarsas and religious institutions, tribal affairs, internal surveillance/ security duties, VIP security duties, minority affairs and anti-terrorism activities. An officer of the rank of Brigadier generally heads each sub-division. However, officers of the rank of Colonels and Majors head some of the lesser units.

The DDG (Pol) continues to function with full blessings of the military dictator and is said to have been tasked to screen the election aspirants, candidates, eliminate the undesirable aspirants either by persuasion or by force and to ensure that the election returns a rubber stamp National Assembly.

The office of the DDG (External I) requires some special mention. It controls the 'foreign operations' of the ISI and presides over the most dreaded wing of the ISI-Counter intelligence. It also covers the territorial, geo-political, economic, strategic intelligence affairs in the Middle East, Africa and other countries. The DDG (External I) also maintains liaison with the PMO (whenever there is one), and with the office of the CMLA/CEO/President, whatever designation a military dictator prefers to decorate himself with. DDG (External I) is a powerful position.

DDG (External II) has the onerous responsibility for coordinating activities of Joint Intelligence M and N, which are India and Kashmir specific. It also supervises and coordinates activities of the Jihadi tanzeems, which do not cross the limit imposed by the Pakistani rulers and draw attention of the US agencies. The operations in Pakistan Occupied Kashmir and the Gilgit and Northern Areas are also looked over by this branch.

With the Al Qaeda and Taliban establishing firm foothold on the NWFP, South and North Waziristan and Chitral Tract, the ISI is called upon to generate intelligence and assist the Army, which is fighting a losing battle in the tribal areas. It has been alleged by US observers that considerable number of rogue and Islamicised ISI and Army personnel were encouraging the Taliban and Al Qaeda forces to establish stronghold in the tribal and frontier areas. The ISI and the Army had brokered a temporary peace with Al Qaeda and the Taliban in South Waziristan in February 2007. However, this brief spell was disturbed after several tribal chieftains joined hands with the Taliban and Al Qaeda forces. Mullah Mehsud apart, the entire Waziri tract is now infested by Taliban and Al Qaeda warriors.

"In recent months, as Musharraf has grown more and more unpopular after eight years of rule, Islamists have been emboldened. The homegrown militants who have hidden Al Qaeda's leaders since the end of 2001 are no longer restricted to untamed mountain villages along the border. These Islamist fighters now operate relatively freely in cities like Karachi—a process the U.S. and Pakistani governments call "Talibanization." Hammered by suicide bombers and Iraq-style IEDs and reluctant to make war on its countrymen, Pakistan's demoralized military seems incapable of stopping the jihadists even in the cities." (Where The Jihad Lives Now—Ron Moreau and Michael Hirsh, *Newsweek,* Oct 19, 2007).

Under these circumstances Pakistani observers have commented that the Al Qaeda and Taliban are happily cohabiting with homegrown jihadis in the interiors of Pakistan's mainland and even in cities like Lahore, Karachi and Islamabad. The ISI, IB and the Army are reluctant to confront them as the lessons of the Lal Masjid incident and loss of over 1500 soldiers in the tribal areas have scared them. Willy nilly the intelligence and security agencies and a section of the army are cooperating with the jihadists. With increasing pressure at home and from the USA for restoration of democracy the ISI, IB and the Army might feel more comfortable with the Talibanised Pakistanis.

With such internal portends the prospects of Pakistan's accelerated thrusts inside Indian mainland, besides the Kashmir, appear to be a certainty. The ISI in collaboration with the Directorate General of Forces Intelligence of Bangladesh (DGFI) are already engaged in promoting jihadist activities in Bangladesh and exporting jihad to India through Al Qaeda, Lashkar-e-Toiba, Jaish-e-Mohammad, Al Badr, HUJI and Jamait-ul-Mujahideen, Bangladesh etc. outfits. These agencies are franchised to carry out blasts and mass killings in India. Pakistan and Bangladesh are merrily perching jihadi footprints in India by opening innumerable modules.

On the other hand of the spectrum the ISI and the DGFI are jointly and severally aiding and supporting the insurgent outfits of Northeast India and certain Muslim separatist organisations. It is estimated that with greater instability in Pakistan and Bangladesh the jihadist forces would succeed in establishing firmer foothold in India. These agencies are not interested and motivated in checkmating jihadist ambience in their own countries. They are being encouraged by international Islamist movements to expand their activities in India, besides defeating the US war against terrorism in Afghanistan, Pakistan and elsewhere in the globe.

The often asked question about the future of Pakistan's Intelligence agencies cannot be answered astrologically. Evolution and reconditioning of these tools of governance would depend on the immediate future political evolution of Pakistan and its geostrategical juxtapositioning alongside its allies like the USA, Saudi Arabia, UK etc.

Internally the Pakistani society is vertically and horizontally divided into three distinct camps: those who aspire and want to achieve true democracy; the fundamentalist and jihadist forces who want Taliban type regime in Pakistan and strong segments of the Armed Forces which want continued military hegemony. With the return of Benazir Bhutto Party and Nawaz Sharif, the democratic forces might coalesce around them and struggle for restoration of democracy. They might get limited cooperation from Pervez Musharraf who is under pressure from the US and other allies to try the democratic façade for strengthening his popular base and mobilising the Pakistani civil society in fighting the Taliban and Al Qaeda forces.

Musharraf has limited manoeuvrability with an elected government demanding his impeachment. Though surrounded by loyal Army Chief, Corps Commanders, and ISI Chiefs Musharraf can count on the loyalty factor as long as the factor hangs on the strings of US support. In Pakistan, loyalty is as amorphous as fast evaporating camphor. No one can rule out another Junta coterie deposing Musharraf and repacking the present democratic government. However, it appears that the tired and exasperated Army is willing to give a limited trial to the US arranged political marriage between democracy and military rule. The immediate range future of Pakistan would depend on the success of this experiment. The civilian government shall have to walk carefully along a multi-edged sword between the military which is the traditional political soul of Pakistan, the jihadist and Islamist forces trying to wrest the soul of Pakistan and the civil society which is expecting too much from a tired political personality who has gained support at home and abroad.

In this scenario the ISI and the IB are likely to cut out fine furrows of their own between the hazardous territories dominated by International Islamic Jihadists, the ambitious leaders of the Armed Forces and the burgeoning expectations of the civil society. These agencies would like to cater to all palates as far as practicable, thus preserving their own identity and interests and swinging along with the wind whichever is stronger.

Minute analysis of the historical threads of the soul of Pakistan Army and the country's jihadist soul and weakened and stunted democratic forces it can be deduced that the Army would not agree to hand over power to the civil society and return to the barracks. The jihadist forces comprising the Taliban, Al Qaeda and home grown tanzeems are not likely to vacate the safe bases in Pakistan. They are likely to strengthen these bases and widen their activities in Afghanistan, Iran, Iraq, and Central Asian countries, India, Bangladesh etc, besides other theatres in West-Asia, Africa, Europe and the Americas. Pakistan is expected to be the strongest base of the Islamic jihadist forces.

Therefore, it would be premature to assume that the Pakistani Intelligence Agencies would disarm themselves and willingly function as appendages to the civilian government. The ISI, MI and the IB are expected to support the jihadists and political hegemony of the Army. They would, in all certainty, continue to escalate jihadist activities inside India. The Indian tools of governance, both civilian and Army should, therefore, remain focussed to the internal developments in Pakistan, Bangladesh, and Afghanistan and tune their security antennae to fight these diabolical forces.

From early 2008, the ISI has come under fresh doubts. Its hands were suspected in the assassination of Benazir Bhutto. ISI links with Afghan Talibans headed by Mullah Omar and Maulvi Haqqani have come under scrutiny. Several Pakistani Taliban groups, namely the ones headed by Baitullah Mehsud and Commander Sadiq are reported to have link with certain groups in the ISI. On the other hand ISI connectivity with Pakistani jihadi tanzeems is alive and the agency continues to direct jihadi attacks inside India.

Under US pressure, especially after it came to notice that July 2008 attack on Indian embassy in Kabul by a fidayeen Taliban was actually masterminded by the ISI, the Pakistan government issued orders transferring the ISI from Defence Ministry to the Interior Ministry. However, under pressure from the Army and the President the order was kept in abeyance and Musharraf came out in blatant support of the spy agency.

Under the circumstances the ISI is likely to accrue power and support the Army in its efforts to dominate the entire panorama of activities in Pakistan.

* * *

11

Preparation for Nuclear Disasters

*BRIG (DR) H K KAR (RETD)**

Count One, Count Two, Count Three .... Are you still in this world ? If you are, the chances are that you may live, but in what condition and for how long is a priceless question. If you are not in this world (wherever you are), you will probably sigh in relief for not being in the area of the holocaust. After all, you have just been evicted from an area devastated by a nuclear bomb. Natural disasters are not new to mankind. In fact, we have also got accustomed to man-made disasters. But a nuclear disaster, created by a planned attack on mankind will be so horrendous that it is unimaginable.

Global experience of the use of nuclear weapons is confined to the two bombs that were dropped in Japan.

---

* Brig (Dr) H K Kar (Retd) was Chief Engineer, Eastern Command

Atom Bombs dropped in Hiroshima and Nagasaki during the Second World War yielded 12.5 Kilotons and 22 Kilotons of energy respectively. 50% of all the deaths were due to burns and about 67% deaths occurred on the first day. 37% people received lethal doze of radiation and those who survived within the radius of half a mile of the explosion died within a week or two. Nuclear bombs have not been used since the Second World War by any country because of their horrendous effects, but ironically, the nuclear powers have been developing more and more powerful nuclear weapons which can destroy the world many times over.

The use of nuclear weapons during a war cannot be ruled out even today, particularly on the pretext of "ending the war" or "saving the honour and prestige of the country". From the consideration of the economics too, nuclear device are less expensive as compared to the cost of munitions, the number of air sorties and the field force required. However, the possibility of an attack with a nuclear warhead in the present day geopolitical scenario is remotely possible. It may happen only if there is a war and that too, when the nuclear capable adversary is likely to face a strategic defeat. However, the possibility of radiological bombs or dirty bombs being used by anti-national elements cannot be ruled out. The possibility of initiating a nuclear disaster by terrorists is much higher than a conventional nuclear attack by another country.

In keeping with the federal structure of the country, responsibility to cope with any disaster is essentially that of the state governments. The role of the Central Government is only supportive in terms of supplementation of physical and financial resources. However, mitigation of the horrendous effects of a nuclear disaster, is way beyond the capacity of the state governments. Not only should the Central Government step in at the very first instance, it is essential that for nuclear disasters a scheme is evolved so that a holistic approach can be taken and contingency plans prepared to mitigate nuclear disaster in the states.

International assistance may also be essential, and hence the plans should include proper reception of such aid, and directing the same to the holocaust area.

In India, the National Disaster Management Authority (NDMA) was created under the Disaster Management Act 2005. NDMA is the lead agency to coordinate the consequences of management of all disasters including nuclear disasters. An interesting aspect of this Act is that the District Disaster Management Authorities are headed by the respective district collectors and co-chaired by elected representatives of the respective districts. In case of a nuclear disaster, the magnitude will be so large that the NDMA will have to take charge at the earliest. A National Disaster Response Force (NDRF) has also been created for specialized response, and has personnel trained to mitigate nuclear disasters.

A nuclear disaster can take place during war, like the dropping of the Atom Bomb at Hiroshima and Nagasaki, by accident like the nuclear incident at Chernobyl or by terrorist and anti-national elements. To be able to mitigate a nuclear disaster, it is essential for the general population to have a broad understanding of the characteristics and how these weapons affect men and materials. The initial devastating phase lasts for about 10-90 seconds. Nuclear weapon detonation is accompanied with the release of huge quantity of energy which is transformed into blast waves, heat and nuclear radiations. Temperatures of over 8000°C is achieved in less than a million of a second. At Hiroshima and Nagasaki the heat was sufficient to burn the exposed human skin at distances as great as 4 Kilometers from ground zero. Many people caught in the open within about 1 to 2 Kilometers from the ground zero were burnt to death but others who were closer, just evaporated. About 15% of the energy yield of a nuclear explosion is given off as ionizing radiation. The initial radiation doze at Hiroshima was of the order of 100,000 RADS whereas the total radiation doze in a person should not exceed 75 RADS.

In a nuclear detonation there will be an extremely bright flash of light several times brighter than the sun, dazzling personnel and causing temporary loss of sight and retinal burns. This will be accompanied by release of heat and followed by a thunderous sound of blast and soon a huge ball of fire brighter than the Sun will be seen rising towards the sky. Gradually this ball of fire would transform into a mushroom cloud. People far away from the site of incident will be able to see, hear and guess what could have happened. Persons near the site of the disaster would not be alive to hear or feel anything. Many would have simply vapourised at the site of the disaster and around, buildings would have collapsed, trapping people below debris, structures would be burning and vehicles would be lying all over and possibly burning. The blast will soon be followed by the falling to earth of radioactive dust, known as nuclear fallout. There will be a haze around the site of the disaster as immediate fallout of the radioactive dust take place. The trees in the area would have been uprooted and sent like missiles causing secondary damages. Burn cases will be very high and the sight of burn and charred bodies or persons with their skin and flesh peeling off from their bodies will be a familiar sight.

The scene of a nuclear disaster will not only traumatize the persons affected in the area but is also likely to traumatize the persons who will visit the site at a later date for providing succour to the casualties and managing the after-effects of the disaster.

Evidence of a nuclear disaster will travel far and wide, without anyone having to inform the concerned authorities. In fact, the district authorities in the area of disaster may cease to exist. Hence, the flash, bang and fireball should start the disaster mitigation machinery of the neighbouring district into gear. The catastrophic impact of a nuclear disaster can only be mitigated through a well coordinated disaster management plan and efficient execution of the same. Some of the essential aspects for disaster mitigation are:

- Comprehensive Disaster Management Plan should be prepared by each District Headquarter in consultation with local bodies, medical, police and firefighting authorities.
- Prior positioning of emergency resources should be done.
- Training of local population and capacity building is of paramount importance. Capacity building is critical at all levels. This is a complex and long term phenomenon that requires the development of human resource. Higher the level of the capacity building, the lower will be the level at which a nuclear disaster can be tackled.
- Rehearsals in the form of simulative exercises to build awareness is of paramount importance.
- Effective use of media to create awareness and broadcast preventive actions to be taken.
- Respond to a nuclear disaster anywhere in the country with utmost speed and efficiency.

Local residents on an emergency situation should use the Incident Command System to ensure that all responders and their support assets are coordinated for effective and efficient response. The incident commander should initially be the senior responder of the organizations like the Chief of Police, Chief of Military, Chief of Fire Service and hand over command to the NDMA through the civil administrator of that area. As with any type of radiation one should reduce the exposure by:

- Shielding, i.e. getting behind thick structure.
- Distancing oneself from the blast and fallout to lessen exposure.
- Minimizing the time spent in the area to reduce the quantum of exposure.

The effects of nuclear or radiological explosion will be similar, though the magnitude of the nuclear explosion will be much larger than the radiological one. If one is caught in the open when a nuclear device explodes one should immediately:

- Drop to the ground and face downwards with the head in the direction of the blast.
- Close eyes and mouth.
- Protect ears with thumbs and cover eyes with palm.
- Keep hands under the body, if unprotected.
- Remain prone until all effects of the explosion have passed and the debris have stopped falling.
- Move under cover/shelter or evacuate upwind of the suspected area.
- If inside buildings and the incident is outside, one must stay inside, turn off all the air conditioners and seal the windows and doors, if possible with plastic tape.

To reduce the effect of radioactive fall-out, the body should be covered as far as possible. Since radio-activity cannot be destroyed, the clothing should be brushed of the dirt and removed. At the earliest opportunity, one should decontaminate oneself by scrubbing and washing with soap and water. In case there are burn injuries, one should try and wet the area in the running water to reduce the temperature and contain the burn.

Unlike most other disasters, where reaching the site of the accident at the earliest instance reduces casualties, in the case of nuclear disasters this will not be true. The police will have to cordon off the area and ensure that only personnel with NBC protective equipment are permitted to proceed anywhere near the site of the disaster. A major requirement in the preparation for nuclear disasters will be that of "personal protective equipment", without which it will not be possible to provide any assistance to the affected people.

Procurement, storage and transshipment to the area of the disaster of personal protective equipment will therefore be a very important facet of preparation for nuclear disasters. Proper rehearsals and simulated exercises should be carried out with regard to casualty management. Photographs of the casualties with identification tags where possible, decontamination of the casualties, segregating contaminated clothing and safe disposal of waste water from casualty decontamination requires special attention.

Preparation of hospitals all over the country to handle the casualties of a nuclear disaster will be a serendipitous effort, since it is likely to meet a lot of resistance. However, in the preparatory stage the basic minimum actions that could be taken are:

- The hospital should be demarcated into Clean Area and Contaminated Area. For example, the closed or covered area may be designated as Clean Area and the open area in front of the Casualty Department (generally the area for parking of cars) could be earmarked as the Contaminated Area, or any other suitable area, preferably in the downwind direction and away from the main hospital building.
- The Contaminated Area should have pre-designated Ambulance Parking Site, Casualty Reception Centre, Regulation Site, Incubation Site and Decontamination Site.
- Simulation exercises must be carried out, not only for the hospital staff, but also personnel of local civil defence organizations, NGOs and if possible local organizations in the area.
- Adequate NBC protective gear like non-permeable disposable decontamination suits, face masks, respirators, canisters, gloves, over-boots etc., must be available for the persons who will be required to work in the contaminated area.

- Medicines and medical kit like fullers earth, hypochlorite solution, soap, scrubbers, spare clothes, towels, non-permeable plastic/polythene bags etc., to treat radiological contaminated casualties and burn casualties should be stored separately and replaced/replenished as the usable date expires.
- Arrangements should be available to convert a portion of the Contaminated Area into Wet Decontamination Site so that the casualties are able to take a shower and decontaminate themselves.

The quicker the flow of the information regarding a nuclear disaster, the faster will be the possibility of taking action to commence mitigation. A database should be created at the national level to include the various organizations to be contacted, the location where disaster relief materials are available, the location of trained manpower, the places where special medicines required for treating nuclear casualties are located etc. The information database should be percolated to all concerned and updated periodically.

Construction of nuclear protection shelters or the use of underground metro subways, could be a major consideration in the preparation for NBC disasters. But would there be adequate time to move into those shelters? In fact, would there be adequate time to think of the response should a nuclear catastrophe take place? Therefore, though pessimistic, preparations will be realistic if planned for taking expeditious action once a nuclear disaster takes place, wherever it takes place .... If such an approach is acceptable the processes that should be given due consideration for preparation are: creating an awareness and broad understanding among the people of the after-effects of a nuclear explosion, training and conducting simulation exercises involving the participation of local bodies, government and non-government organizations and the common people in the mitigation of nuclear disasters, procurement of adequate quantities of NBC protective equipment and locating them at various nodal points, ensuring that all hospitals have plans as well as wherewithal to provide medical assistance to nuclear contaminated casualties, and last but not the least, the media should be incorporated in the training process to understand the mechanism of mitigation of a nuclear disaster.

* * *

Index